Multilingual Mentality:

Strategies for Learning Multiple Languages Simultaneously

HARLAN G. OTIS

OTIS
PUBLISHING

First published by Otis Publishing 2024

Copyright © 2024

First edition

1

Introduction

Did you know that polyglots, or individuals who master multiple languages, often showcase enhanced brain structures and superior cognitive abilities?

It's true!

Studies have shown that juggling more than one language can sharpen your mind, improve multitasking skills, and even delay the onset of dementia.

This book is your ticket to understanding and leveraging these fascinating neurological benefits by learning languages simultaneously. We dive into how to make the most of your brain's incredible capacity to juggle languages, offering practical strategies that anyone can apply.

With years of practice and a passion for languages that knows no bounds, I crafted this book to guide you on a similar journey of discovery and growth. Unlike other language learning guides, this book marries scientific research with real-life applications. Its blend of personal insights, motivational stories, and actionable strategies is designed to help you navigate the waters of simultaneous language learning. This unique approach promises fluency in multiple languages and a deeper appreciation for the cognitive marvels of the multilingual mind.

What can you expect from diving into these pages? A comprehensive understanding of the cognitive benefits of learning multiple languages at once, effective and practical strategies for doing so, and tips for overcoming the hurdles that might come your way.

This book is crafted for a broad audience - whether you're a teen just starting, an adult looking to expand your linguistic repertoire, or somewhere in between, there's something here for you. Structured to take you from the foundational aspects of the multilingual mind to advanced strategies for personal development as a polyglot, this journey we're about to undertake together is nothing short of transformative.

So, if you're ready to challenge your language learning paradigms and unlock new levels of cognitive prowess, you've come to the right place. Let's embark on this exciting adventure with an open mind and a heart full of determination.

Let's turn the page and start this enriching journey together.

2

Chapter 1: The Human Brain

In the labyrinth of the human mind, language acts not just as a means of communication but as the architect of our cognitive structures, shaping how we perceive and interact with the world. Learning languages, especially multiple languages simultaneously, serves as a testament to the brain's remarkable capability to adapt and thrive under complex and dynamic demands.

This chapter explores the profound impact multilingualism has on neural pathways, showcasing how the brain's plasticity, connectivity, cognitive reserve, and efficiency are not just enhanced but are fundamentally transformed in the process.

The Brain on Multiple Languages: How Multilingualism Shapes Our Neural Pathways

Brain Plasticity

Brain plasticity, or neuroplasticity, refers to the brain's ability to reorganize itself by forming new neural connections throughout life. This ability is at the heart of language learning. When one undertakes to learn new languages, they're not merely memorizing words and grammar rules; they're engaging in cognitive restructuring. This restructuring enhances the brain's plasticity, making it more adept at adapting to new challenges. For instance, when a person practices speaking a new language, they forge and reinforce pathways in the brain. These pathways can be leveraged for various cognitive tasks beyond language learning.

A Swedish Armed Forces Interpreter Academy study observed individuals undergoing intensive language learning courses. The results, published in "NeuroImage," revealed significant structural changes in participants' brains, not observed in control groups. These findings underscore the tangible impact of language learning on brain structure, particularly in areas associated with learning and spatial navigation.

Enhanced Connectivity

Learning multiple languages also enhances the connectivity between different regions of the brain. This increased connectivity improves overall brain function, manifesting in various cognitive benefits such as better problem-solving skills and enhanced memory. When you learn a new language, your brain must create connections between seemingly disparate pieces of information – the sound of a word, its meaning, its grammatical role – and integrate them into your existing cognitive framework. This process strengthens the connections within specific brain language areas and across different cognitive areas, fostering a more interconnected, efficient neural network.

Research from the University of Edinburgh and Nizwa University in Oman found that bilingual individuals show increased connectivity in the brain's white matter pathways, particularly in language processing and executive control regions. This enhanced connectivity contributes to the cognitive flexibility observed in multilingual individuals, allowing them to switch between tasks more efficiently.

Cognitive Reserve

Cognitive reserve refers to the brain's resilience to neuropathological damage. A higher cognitive reserve means a more remarkable ability to withstand the impacts of aging and brain diseases such as dementia and Alzheimer's. Multilingualism plays a significant role in building this cognitive reserve. By constantly engaging in the complex task of language learning and usage, multilingual individuals create a buffer for their brain, enhancing its ability to function even when faced with potential damage.

A pivotal study published in the journal "Neurology" found that bilingual and multilingual Alzheimer's patients manifested symptoms of the disease an average of 4.5 years later than monolingual patients. This delay is a testament to the protective effects of multilingualism on cognitive health, providing compelling evidence for the role of language learning in bolstering cognitive reserve.

Neural Efficiency

Lastly, the efficiency with which bilingual and multilingual brains operate is significantly higher compared to monolingual brains. This efficiency is observed in how multilingual individuals process information, using fewer resources during language tasks. When you learn multiple languages, your brain becomes adept at filtering out irrelevant information and focusing on what's important, a skill that translates to increased efficiency in cognitive processing across the board.

A study by the University of Pompeu Fabra in Spain showed that multilingual individuals have a heightened ability to monitor their environment and switch their attention when necessary.

6

This ability indicates a more efficient use of neural resources as the brain learns to juggle multiple languages.

The journey into multilingualism is not just about adding languages to your repertoire but fundamentally enhancing how your brain functions. Through the lens of neuroplasticity, connectivity, cognitive reserve, and neural efficiency, we begin to appreciate the profound and multifaceted impact of learning multiple languages on our mental architecture.

Becoming multilingual is akin to a workout for the brain, one that equips it with the flexibility, resilience, and efficiency necessary to navigate the complexities of the modern world. As we delve deeper into the strategies and practices of simultaneous language learning, remember that with each new language, you're not just learning to communicate in another tongue – you're sculpting a more robust, agile, and interconnected mind.

Cognitive Advantages of Being Multilingual: Beyond Language Learning

Multilingualism offers cognitive dividends far beyond the mere ability to converse in multiple tongues. Juggling languages primes the brain for a suite of enhanced cognitive functions, making the multilingual individual adept at navigating the complexities of modern life with enviable agility.

Improved Attention Control

Multilingual individuals exhibit remarkable prowess on the battlefield of attention, where distractions vie for supremacy. The constant mental gymnastics of switching between languages endow them with refined control over their attentional resources. This is not merely an academic observation but a lived reality for those who manage multiple linguistic codes daily. They find themselves better equipped to filter out irrelevant stimuli, which is invaluable in a world of information overload.

Consider the scenario of a professional immersed in a multilingual workplace. Here, the ability to focus amidst a cacophony of languages becomes an asset and a necessity. This individual, through the very practice of language juggling, hones an attentional control that allows for a seamless transition between tasks, languages, and cultural nuances, turning potential chaos into a symphony of productivity.

Enhanced Memory Abilities

The corridors of memory, too, are widened and reinforced in the multilingual mind. Memorizing vocabulary, syntax, and the subtleties of multiple languages serves as a rigorous exercise regimen for the brain, enhancing its capacity to store and retrieve information. This is akin to a mental form of cross-training, where the brain's memory muscles are flexed

8

across various tasks, leading to overall improvements in memory function.

Language learners often employ structured and strategic memory exercises, such as mnemonic devices, spaced repetition, and leveraging linguistic similarities, to aid in retaining new languages. While developed within the context of language learning, these techniques have broader applications, enhancing the individual's ability to remember names, facts, and sequences outside the realm of languages. The disciplined application of these memory strategies transforms the mundane act of memorization into a tool for cognitive enhancement, offering benefits that permeate all areas of life.

Problem-Solving Skills

Decoding and encoding in multiple languages instills mental flexibility, a skill of thought that is the hallmark of an adept problem solver. Multilingual individuals accustomed to navigating the complexities of different linguistic structures develop an enhanced ability to see problems from multiple perspectives and devise innovative solutions. This mental agility is not confined to linguistic gymnastics but extends to the broader canvas of life's challenges.

Switching between languages requires not just linguistic but cultural fluency, understanding how things are said and why they are said in a certain way. This deep engagement with diverse modes of thinking cultivates a problem-solving approach that is both creative and analytical, capable of traversing the boundaries between disparate ideas to synthesize novel solutions. This capacity for complex problem-solving is invaluable in a world where challenges seldom present themselves linearly and monolingually.

Creativity Boost

Finally, the kaleidoscopic experience of multilingualism acts as a catalyst for creativity. At its core, exposure to multiple languages is exposure to various ways of seeing the world. Each language, with its unique metaphors, idioms, and expressions, offers a new lens through which to view reality. This diversity of perspectives is fertile ground for creativity, encouraging divergent thinking and exploring ideas beyond conventional boundaries.

The creative benefits of multilingualism manifest in various domains, from artistic expression to scientific innovation. The multilingual mind, adept at drawing connections between seemingly unrelated concepts, is well-equipped to venture into the uncharted territories of creativity. Whether in writing, art, or problem-solving, thinking outside the conventional confines of a single linguistic and cultural perspective fuels innovation and originality.

The cognitive advantages of being multilingual unfold across the spectrum of mental functions, from sharp attentional control and robust memory to dynamic problem-solving and boundless creativity. These abilities, honed in the crucible of language learning, equip individuals with the tools to excel in their personal and professional lives and navigate the complexities of a rapidly changing world with grace and agility. Multilingualism is not merely a linguistic achievement but a comprehensive cognitive enhancement, enriching the mind in profound and enduring ways.

The Myths of the 'Critical Period' for Language Learning Debunked

Long-held beliefs in the language learning sphere often paint a picture of a fleeting window of opportunity, the so-called 'critical period,' beyond which the brain supposedly loses its linguistic elasticity, making new language acquisition a near-impossible feat for adults. This profoundly ingrained yet widely contested myth presumes a rigidity of the adult mind that research and real-world experience continually refute. The truth, illuminated by a growing body of neuroscientific evidence, tells a different story—one of enduring neuroplasticity, where the capacity for linguistic assimilation spans well beyond the early years into adulthood and even later life.

Rather than succumbing to a state of stagnation post-childhood, the brain maintains a remarkable capacity for learning anew, adapting its neural architecture in response to new linguistic environments and challenges. This capacity for continuous learning, far from being confined to the language domain, reflects a broader cognitive flexibility that characterizes the human brain throughout its life. Adults stepping into multiple languages do not find themselves at the mercy of a diminished neural plasticity; instead, they encounter a brain still ripe for transformation, capable of forging and strengthening the synaptic connections that underpin language proficiency.

Adult language acquisition, while distinct in its trajectory compared to children's, is far from a romantic pursuit. With a wealth of life experience and an arsenal of learning strategies, adults approach language learning with a sophistication and purpose that can accelerate the journey to fluency. They wield the tools of critical thinking, metacognitive awareness, and strategic planning—tools that allow for a more structured and self-directed path to language mastery. These strategies, ranging from the systematic application of spaced repetition to the deliberate practice of conversational skills, harness the adult learner's cognitive resources to align with their learning objectives, lifestyle, and motivation.

Moreover, once underestimated, the adult brain's capacity for neuroplasticity has been illuminated by recent research, revealing an adaptability that extends well into later stages of life. This neuroplasticity, the brain's ability to rewire itself in response to learning and experience, underpins the adult's capacity to acquire new languages. Studies employing neuroimaging techniques have shown that even in adulthood, engaging in language learning activities stimulates brain structure and function changes akin to those observed in younger learners. This neural adaptability ensures that the adult brain remains fertile for linguistic enrichment, challenging the notion that language learning is an endeavor best left to the young.

Adults possess a strategic advantage in language acquisition in this landscape of continuous learning capability and sustained neuroplasticity. This advantage springs not from a purportedly superior innate capacity for language learning but from the depth and breadth of their life experiences. Adults bring to language learning a rich tapestry of prior knowledge, cognitive skills, and cultural insights that can be leveraged to facilitate the understanding and assimilation of new languages. They are adept at drawing parallels between their native and target languages, applying mnemonic techniques honed in professional or academic contexts, and deploying metacognitive strategies to monitor and optimize their learning process. This ability to draw upon diverse cognitive resources and experiences endows the adult learner with a multifaceted toolkit for language learning, one that can be tailored to their unique learning preferences and goals.

Far from being a hindrance, the adult's journey into multilingualism is enriched by the factors presumed to constrain it. The narrative of language learning as a domain exclusive to the young is steadily being dismantled, replaced by a recognition of the lifelong capacity for linguistic growth and the unique advantages adults bring to this endeavor. In debunking the myths of the critical period, we uncover a more nuanced understanding of language learning—one that celebrates the brain's enduring adaptability and the strategic knowledge of the adult learner.

Polyglot Brains: What We Can Learn from the World's Most Proficient Language Learners

In polyglots, where the mastery of multiple languages interweaves with the fabric of daily life, a treasure trove of methodologies, cognitive strategies, and personal drives unveils itself. Through their journey across the landscapes of numerous tongues, these linguistic virtuosos offer insights that extend far beyond the confines of language learning; they present a blueprint for cognitive enhancement, adaptability, and sustained motivation.

Learning Strategies

At the heart of polyglot efficacy lie the learning strategies, a collection of practices refined through years of linguistic exploration. These strategies, while diverse, share common threads of immersion, contextual learning, and the strategic use of technology. Polyglots, for instance, often immerse themselves in the language not through traditional study alone but by integrating the new language into their daily activities. This might involve changing the language settings on their devices, engaging with media in the target language, or even setting aside periods where only the new language is spoken. Such immersion creates a necessity, a linguistic environment that demands understanding and active use of the language, thereby accelerating proficiency.

Moreover, polyglots leverage contextual learning, understanding that language is not just a system of rules but a living, breathing entity within a culture. They seek to learn languages in situ, using them as tools to gain insights into the cultures, histories, and philosophies of those who speak them. This approach transforms language learning from a mere academic exercise into an enriching exploration of human diversity.

Technology, too, plays a pivotal role in polyglot strategies. From spaced repetition systems that optimize memory retention to language exchange platforms that connect learners across the globe, polyglots utilize a range of digital tools to complement their learning. These technologies allow for a personalized learning experience, enabling learners to focus on their areas of need while providing the flexibility to learn anytime, anywhere.

Mental Organization

The ability of polyglots to navigate multiple linguistic terrains without succumbing to confusion stems from their adept mental organization. This organization involves compartmentalizing each language, a cognitive strategy allowing efficient access and use. Far from being a rigid boundary, this compartmentalization is fluid, with polyglots able to easily switch between languages, a phenomenon known as code-switching. This mental agility is cultivated through practice, with polyglots often engaging in exercises requiring rapid switching between languages, enhancing their ability to maintain clear boundaries between linguistic systems.

Motivational Factors

Underpinning the polyglot's journey is a mosaic of motivational factors, each contributing to the sustained pursuit of multilingualism. For many, the drive stems from a deep-seated curiosity about the world, a desire to connect with others in their native tongues, and a quest for personal growth. This intrinsic motivation, fueled by the joy of discovery and the satisfaction of overcoming linguistic challenges, propels learners forward, even in the face of obstacles. Additionally, extrinsic factors, such as professional aspirations or the practical benefits of multilingualism, offer tangible rewards for linguistic proficiency.

Polyglots create a self-reinforcing motivation cycle by intertwining their passions and interests with their language learning. Whether driven by a love for literature, a passion for travel, or the desire to forge meaningful connections across cultures, they find ways to align their language learning with their broader life goals, acquiring new languages as a deeply integrated aspect of their identity.

Adaptability and Flexibility

The polyglot's path is marked by exceptional adaptability and flexibility, qualities that extend beyond language learning to influence their broader cognitive and emotional resilience. This adaptability is evident in their approach to learning, where rigid methodologies give way to a more fluid, responsive engagement with languages. Polyglots are not wedded using a single method. Still, they are continually adjusting their strategies based on their evolving needs, the languages they are learning, and the contexts in which they use them.

This flexibility is also reflected in their cognitive style. Polyglots, accustomed to the mental gymnastics of navigating multiple grammatical systems and vocabularies, develop cognitive flexibility that enhances their problem-solving abilities, creativity, and critical thinking capacity. They view languages not as separate silos but as interconnected systems, a perspective that allows them to draw on their entire linguistic repertoire to learn new languages more efficiently.

In essence, the world's most proficient language learners embody a model of cognitive and emotional resilience that transcends the realm of language learning through their strategies, mental organization, motivational drivers, and adaptability. Their journey offers valuable lessons for aspiring polyglots and anyone seeking to enhance their mental capabilities, adaptability, and lifelong learning potential.

The Role of Memory in Language Learning: Techniques for Enhancement

In its labyrinthine complexity, memory serves as the foundation upon which the edifice of language learning is built. Its capacity to retain, recall, and reconfigure linguistic elements underpins our ability to assimilate and utilize new languages. Within this cognitive framework, specific methodologies stand out for their efficacy in enhancing memory, transforming the nebulous task of language acquisition into a structured, manageable endeavor.

Spaced Repetition Systems (SRS)

At the forefront of these methodologies is the utilization of Spaced Repetition Systems (SRS), a technique that optimizes the consolidation of linguistic knowledge by strategically timing review sessions. This system operates on the principle of the forgetting curve, a concept that delineates how information is lost over time when there is no attempt to retain it. By revisiting language elements at increasing intervals, SRS counteracts the natural decay of memory, ensuring that vocabulary and grammar are not just learned but ingrained. The elegance of SRS lies in its adaptability; it gauges the learner's mastery of each item, adjusting the review schedule to focus on areas that require reinforcement. This personalized approach ensures that the vast tapestry of a new language is committed to memory with an efficiency that traditional repetition learning methods cannot match.

Mnemonic Devices

Complementing the systematic approach of SRS are mnemonic devices, tools that create a scaffold for memory by weaving connections between new linguistic elements and pre-existing knowledge. These devices range from simple acronyms to complex narratives, each anchoring the foreign in the familiar. For instance, associating the Spanish word for cat, "Gato," with the image of a cat wearing a hat shaped like a 'G' leverages visual and conceptual associations to enhance recall. By engaging multiple cognitive pathways, such mnemonics facilitate the initial memorization of vocabulary and bolster long-term retention. They transform the abstract into the tangible, embedding new words and phrases within a web of associations that render them accessible and memorable.

Visualization Techniques

Further enriching this mnemonic arsenal are visualization techniques, strategies that employ the mind's eye to create vivid, sensory-rich images of linguistic elements. This method, drawing on the brain's inherent capacity for visual processing, encodes language in a form that is both engaging and memorable. When a learner visualizes a"market" as a bustling, colorful bazaar packed with haggling spices, the word transcends its phonetic structure to evoke a multisensory experience. Such visualization not only aids in memorizing vocabulary but also in comprehending cultural nuances, embedding language learning within a richer, more nuanced cognitive and emotional context.

Contextual Learning

The final pillar supporting memory architecture in language learning is contextual learning, a process that embeds linguistic elements within the fabric of real-life experiences and interactions. This approach recognizes that language is more than a collection of words and rules; it is a vehicle for expression, communication, and connection. By learning a language in context, whether through conversations with native speakers, immersion experiences, or engagement with authentic media, learners anchor linguistic elements in situations that imbue them with meaning. This facilitates memory by creating emotional and situational associations and enhances the learner's ability to deploy language in practical, real-world scenarios. For instance, ordering food in a restaurant becomes a dynamic language-learning exercise that integrates vocabulary, grammar, and cultural etiquette into a cohesive, memorable experience.

Together, these techniques form a comprehensive strategy for enhancing memory in language learning. Spaced Repetition Systems (SRS) ensure that linguistic elements are reviewed optimally to foster deep, lasting retention. Mnemonic devices create a network of associations that anchor new words and phrases in the learner's pre-existing knowledge, making them readily retrievable. Visualization techniques leverage the brain's visual processing capabilities to encode language in a vivid and memorable manner. Finally, contextual learning grounds linguistic elements in real-life experiences, enriching memory with emotional and situational associations. Through the synergy of these methodologies, the daunting task of memorizing the multifaceted components of a new language is rendered not just manageable but deeply enriching, laying the foundation for a robust, enduring proficiency in multiple languages.

Overcoming the Fear of Mixing Languages: Strategies for Clear Segmentation

In the pursuit of multilingualism, a joint apprehension surfaces among learners to blend languages, obscuring the distinct features that define them. While rooted in genuine concern for linguistic purity, this fear overlooks the inherent adaptability and resilience of the cognitive processes underpinning language learning. The strategies delineated here aim not to erect impenetrable barriers between languages but to nurture a mental landscape where each language flourishes, distinct yet harmoniously coexisting.

Language Separation Techniques

The endeavor to maintain linguistic segregation within the mind's confines embarks on a nuanced approach that acknowledges the brain's capacity for compartmentalization. This skill, often unconsciously employed in managing various aspects of daily life, can be refined and directed toward language. Techniques such as assigning different languages to specific days of the week or dedicating particular notebooks for writing in each language serve as tactile and visual cues, reinforcing the separateness of each linguistic system. This methodical delineation encourages the mind to switch gears, so to speak, activating the neural networks associated with the language in focus while momentarily quieting those tied to others.

Contextual Usage

A potent catalyst for the mental segregation of languages lies in their contextual application, a practice that mirrors the natural acquisition processes observed in native bilingual speakers. By reserving specific languages for distinct spheres of interaction—the domestic domain, the professional workspace, or social media platforms—a spatial and situational framework is established that cues the mind to retrieve the appropriate linguistic resources. This strategy does not merely simulate the environmental immersion pivotal to language acquisition but roots each language in a tangible context, enhancing both recall and fluency. Speaking one language at home and another at work, for instance, does not merely prevent linguistic cross-contamination but infuses each language with a unique set of associations, enriching the learner's linguistic experience.

Focused Practice Sessions

The path to linguistic clarity further unfolds through focused practice sessions and deliberate immersion intervals in a single language, free from the intrusion of others. This approach, akin to deep work sessions in the realm of productivity, allows for an intensive engagement with the language, fostering a depth of learning that surface-level multitasking cannot achieve. During these sessions, the language in focus becomes the sole occupant of the cognitive foreground, with all resources directed toward its exploration. The key to the effectiveness of this strategy lies in its regularity; consistent, dedicated practice sessions build a robust familiarity and comfort with each language, gradually diminishing the likelihood of unintentional blending.

Acceptance of Code-Switching

Amid these strategies for linguistic separation, an essential shift in perspective beckons: recognizing code-switching not as a failure but as a natural, even beneficial, facet of multilingualism. This phenomenon, characterized by the fluid alternation between languages within a single discourse reflects not a deficit in linguistic competence but a sophisticated interplay of cognitive skills. Far from being a sign of confusion, code-switching often emerges in contexts requiring nuanced expression, where the languages at a speaker's disposal are leveraged to convey meaning with greater precision, emotional resonance, or cultural relevance. Accepting and embracing code-switching as a legitimate linguistic strategy allows learners to navigate their multilingual identities more easily and authentically. It acknowledges the dynamic nature of language itself, a force not contained neatly within discrete boundaries but flowing, adapting, and intermingling according to communication needs.

In navigating the challenges of learning multiple languages simultaneously, one encounters not just the technical complexities of grammar, vocabulary, and pronunciation but the intricate dance of cognitive processes that underlie linguistic proficiency. The strategies outlined here—the meticulous segregation of languages through practical techniques, the strategic use of contextual cues, the commitment to focused practice, and the acceptance of code-switching as a natural component of language use—collectively forge a path towards confident multilingualism. They acknowledge the brain's remarkable capacity for adaptation, harnessing its potential not just to store and retrieve multiple languages but to do so with a grace that respects the distinctness of each.

In this endeavor, the learner is both an architect and a gardener, meticulously designing the cognitive landscape in which languages are planted and nurtured to maturity. While understandable, the fear of mixing the languages gives way to a confident command over multiple tongues, each finding its place within the tapestry of the mind. This journey, marked by deliberate strategy and open-hearted acceptance, reveals the true potential of the multilingual mind: not a battleground of competing languages but a harmonious symphony of diverse voices, each contributing its unique timbre to the richness of human communication.

The Power of Immersion: Why Full Engagement Is Key to Language Mastery

Immersion, in its most potent form, offers a crucible for linguistic transformation, a space where the boundaries between the learner and the language blur, fostering a deep, intuitive understanding. Far from passive absorption, this process demands active engagement with the language in all its complexity, from the nuanced turns of phrases to the subtle cues of body language accompanying speech. Within this immersive context, language ceases to be a mere academic subject and becomes a living, breathing entity, a medium through which the learner interacts with the world.

Creating immersive environments, particularly outside the country where the target language is spoken, might seem daunting, yet it is within the grasp of any determined learner. The home, a familiar and controlled space, can transform into a linguistic laboratory where the target language infiltrates every corner. Simple adjustments, such as changing the language settings on electronic devices, streaming media in the target language or labeling household items with their corresponding foreign words can steep the learner in the language. Beyond the confines of the home, the community offers a broader canvas for immersion. Language cafes, cultural festivals, and conversation groups provide opportunities for interaction, allowing the learner to practice and refine their language skills in a dynamic, real-world context.

Cultural immersion extends the concept of language learning beyond the spoken and written word, diving into the customs, traditions, and social norms that underpin the language. This holistic approach recognizes that language is not just a tool for communication but a reflection of the culture from which it springs. By engaging with the culture behind the language— be it through cuisine, literature, film, or music—the learner gains insights into the mindset and values of its speakers. Such cultural engagements make the language come alive, transforming abstract vocabulary and grammar rules into expressions of a people's identity and way of life. Through this cultural lens, the learner becomes more proficient in the language and develops a deeper, more empathetic connection with its speakers.

Active participation is the cornerstone of immersive learning, the force that cements the learner's engagement with the language. It is one thing to listen to or read in the target language, absorbing its rhythms and patterns passively; it is another to speak it to use as a tool for expressing thoughts, desires, and emotions. This active use of the language, fraught though it may be with mistakes and misunderstandings, is where authentic learning happens.

In the attempt to communicate, to make oneself understood and to understand in turn, the learner internalizes the language, making it a part of their cognitive and emotional landscape. Conversation partners, whether peers, tutors, or strangers, become collaborators in this process, offering corrections, encouragement, and insight and turning the act of speaking into a dialogue between individuals and cultures.

In this environment of full engagement, language mastery evolves from a distant goal to an immediate, lived experience. The learner, immersed in the language and its culture, engaged in active participation and conversation, moves beyond the role of the student to become a participant in a wider linguistic community. Through immersion, language learning transcends the confines of textbooks and classrooms, transforming into a vibrant, holistic journey of discovery.

Customizing Your Learning Path: Tailoring Strategies to Fit Your Cognitive Style

In language acquisition, a nuanced understanding of one's inherent learning style is a reflective exercise and a strategic foundation for effective, personalized learning strategies. Recognizing whether one's strengths lie in visual, auditory, reading/writing, or kinesthetic modalities paves the way for a learning journey that aligns with individual cognitive preferences and is significantly more rewarding.

For the visual learner, language becomes a tapestry of images and symbols, where flashcards blossom into vibrant mnemonics, and the intricate alphabets of foreign tongues transform into captivating puzzles awaiting solutions. This learner thrives in an environment rich with charts, infographics, and videos that render abstract linguistic concepts into concrete visual representations. Here, the nuances of verb conjugation or the subtleties of tonal languages are not merely textual information but visual patterns to be decoded, making language learning intuitive and engaging.

Conversely, the auditory learner navigates the landscape of language through the rhythm and melody of speech, where the rise and fall of intonation paint aural portraits of meaning. For them, language acquisition flourishes in the echo of dialogues, the cadence of poetry, and the lyricism of songs. This learner finds solace in the spoken word, leveraging podcasts, audio courses, and spoken interactions as primary vehicles for language immersion. The sounds of a new language, from its most straightforward greetings to its most complex debates, become audible content and a symphony of phonetic patterns to be internalized, allowing the learner to attune their ear to the music inherent in every language.

In contrast, the reading/writing learner finds their stride within the realm of text, where language is a landscape to be navigated one word at a time. Articles, books, and written exercises become the soil where their linguistic capabilities flourish. This learner engages with the language through the written word, finding in the act of writing a powerful tool for memorization and practice. The structured nature of written language, with its visible form and tangible presence, provides a solid framework upon which the learner can build their understanding, acquiring vocabulary, grammar, and syntax through deliberate construction.

Meanwhile, the kinesthetic learner approaches language as an embodied experience, where the physicality of speech and the tactile aspects of writing serve as primary conduits for learning. This learner thrives in environments where language is seen or heard and acted out, where role-playing, hands-on activities, and real-world interactions transform abstract linguistic concepts into concrete experiences. For them, the path to language mastery is paved with movement, engaging the body as a powerful learning instrument. The kinesthetic learner seeks to inhabit the language, to feel its rhythms and contours through gesture and action, making the learning process an immersive, physical journey.

Upon this foundation of understanding one's cognitive style, the construction of personalized learning strategies emerges as a dynamic process that requires initial customization and ongoing adaptation. Creating flexible learning plans that accommodate individual lifestyles, preferences, and learning paces becomes beneficial and essential. This flexibility allows the learner to navigate the inevitable ebbs and flows of motivation and progress, adjusting the intensity, focus, and study methods to reflect their current circumstances and goals. Such plans are not static edicts but living documents, evolving with the learner's journey, ensuring that language acquisition remains a vibrant, engaging process.

Integral to this adaptive approach is the establishment of iterative feedback loops, mechanisms through which learners regularly assess their progress, reflect on their strategies, and make necessary adjustments. These feedback loops, whether through self-assessment, interaction with peers or instructors, or digital tools that track and analyze learning patterns, serve as a critical compass guiding the learner's journey. They provide a snapshot of current proficiency and a roadmap for future growth, highlighting areas of strength to be leveraged and challenges to be addressed. This continuous reflection and adjustment process ensures that the learner's strategies remain aligned with their objectives, optimizing the efficacy of their study and accelerating their path to language mastery.

Customizing one's learning path according to cognitive style, adopting flexible learning plans, and incorporating iterative feedback loops are pillars of a practical, personalized approach to navigating the multifaceted terrain of language learning. These elements, woven together, create a tapestry of strategies that accommodate and celebrate the learner's individuality, transforming the challenge of language acquisition into an adventure uniquely tailored to their cognitive landscape.

3

Chapter 2: Sculpting Your Path to Multilingualism

In the vast expanse of language learning, setting precise goals is akin to plotting coordinates on a map, guiding the sojourner through uncharted territories with clarity and purpose. This initial step, seemingly mundane, is imbued with the power to transform aspirations into tangible outcomes, rendering the abstract contours of ambition into measurable landmarks. Therefore, goal-setting is not merely a preliminary task but a foundational stone in the edifice of language mastery.

Defining Your Language Learning Goals: A Tailored Approach

Goal Specificity

Imagine planting a garden where each seed represents a linguistic goal. Just as a gardener selects seeds based on the soil's characteristics, climate, and desired harvest, language learners must also choose their goals with precision and foresight. Specific, Measurable, Attainable, Relevant, and Time-bound (SMART) goals serve as the gardener's tools, ensuring that each linguistic seed has the potential to flourish. For instance, rather than a nebulous aim to "become fluent," a SMART goal might be "to hold a 15-minute conversation in Spanish about daily routines within six months." This specificity provides a clear target and a metric for progress and success.

Long-term vs. Short-term Goals

The balance between immediate milestones and ultimate language proficiency aspirations mirrors the rhythm of a symphony, where short-term goals are the individual notes that, when played in succession, culminate in the grandeur of long-term achievement. This balance ensures that motivation is maintained through regular accomplishments while the overarching objective remains in sight. For example, daily vocabulary learning can serve as a stepping stone toward the broader aim of reading a novel in its original language. Each short-term success is a note in the melody leading toward the symphonic climax of linguistic proficiency.

Personal Relevance

The alignment of language learning goals with personal interests, career aspirations, or cultural connections infuses the process with meaning, transforming it from a task into a passion. When a language learner chooses to study Japanese not just for its linguistic appeal but to connect with their heritage or to engage deeply with a beloved genre of literature, the language becomes a bridge to personal identity and cultural understanding. This personal relevance is a wellspring of motivation, sustaining the learner's enthusiasm and commitment even when challenges arise.

Goal Flexibility

Adaptability in goal-setting is akin to an improvisational dance, where the dancer responds to the music's ebb and flow with fluidity and grace. As language learners progress, encounter obstacles, or discover new interests, the flexibility to adjust their goals ensures that their learning path remains aligned with their evolving desires and circumstances. This might mean shifting focus from one language to another based on changing career needs or modifying proficiency targets to reflect realistic progress rates. Such adaptability fosters resilience and ensures that the language learning process remains responsive to the learner's life, evolving as a reflection of their journey.

Textual Element: Goal-Setting Framework

To crystallize these concepts into actionable steps, consider the following goal-setting framework, designed to guide you in sculpting your personalized path to multilingualism:

1. Define Your SMART Goals: Detail specific, measurable, attainable, relevant, and time-bound goals for each language you wish to learn.
2. Balance Your Aspirations: Outline both short-term milestones and long-term objectives, ensuring they harmonize to support your ultimate aim of language mastery.
3. Align With Your Passions: Connect each goal with personal interests, career aspirations, or cultural explorations, infusing your language learning journey with personal significance.
4. Embrace Flexibility: Periodically reassess your goals, adjusting them to reflect your progress, challenges, and evolving interests.

When applied with thoughtful consideration and regular reflection, this framework serves not just as a roadmap but as a compass, orienting your language learning voyage towards success and fulfillment.

In meticulously crafting language learning goals, the learner embarks not on a predetermined route but on a journey of discovery. Each goal serves as a beacon, illuminating the path toward linguistic proficiency and cultural connection. Through the strategic interplay of specificity, balance, personal relevance, and adaptability, these goals transform from mere aspirations into stepping stones, guiding the learner through the multifaceted landscape of multilingualism.

The Ideal Language Learning Environment: Crafting Your Multilingual Nook

In the pursuit of multilingual proficiency, the sanctity of one's learning environment emerges not as a mere backdrop but as a catalyst, potent in its ability to either propel or impede the voyage toward linguistic mastery. This meticulously cultivated sanctum transcends the ordinary, morphing into a crucible where the alchemy of language learning unfolds. Here, amidst the confluence of physical space setup, resource accessibility, environmental cues, and ergonomic design, lies the heart of a bespoke multilingual nook, a haven meticulously engineered to nurture the seeds of linguistic diversity.

Physical Space Setup

Venturing into the realm of physical space setup, one confronts the challenge of transforming mundane confines into a bastion of inspiration and creativity. The alchemy lies in the deliberate orchestration of elements that, in their harmony, conjure an ambiance conducive to deep, focused study. Illumination, straddling the delicate balance between the warm embrace of ambient lighting and the stark clarity of task lights become a pivotal player in this transformation. Simultaneously, the choice of color palette, favoring serene hues that whisper tranquility yet invigorate the spirit, sets the stage for a journey inward into the depths of language exploration. The strategic placement of furniture ensures a clear, unobstructed flow of energy, inviting the learner to surrender to the embrace of discovery.

Resource Accessibility

The ligaments that bind this sanctuary's potential are the tendrils of resource accessibility. This network ensures that every tool, every time, and every digital artifact lies within the effortless grasp of the seeker. Envision shelves, their arms outstretched, cradling the weight of dictionaries, grammar guides, and literary works, each a beacon calling out to the curious mind. This tangible library, complemented by the digital expanse of applications, podcasts, and online forums, forms a lattice of knowledge that is omnipresent and omnipotent. The meticulous organization of these resources, categorized not by the arbitrary whims of alphabetization but by the intuitive logic of frequency and relevance, ensures that reaching for a tool is as fluid as thought, eliminating barriers between curiosity and enlightenment.

Environmental Cues

Amidst this carefully constructed ecosystem, environmental cues emerge as silent narrators of culture and language. These artifacts, ranging from the subtlety of a wall adorned with foreign scripts to the tactile presence of cultural artifacts, serve as constant, unspoken reminders of the linguistic worlds awaiting discovery. Incorporating such elements beautifies the space and embeds it with a narrative depth, transforming passive surroundings into active participants in the language learning odyssey. Each object, be it a traditional tea set or a map delineated with the contours of distant lands, whispers stories of faraway places and peoples, igniting the imagination and fueling the desire to explore the languages that give voice to these narratives.

Comfort and Ergonomics

Yet, for all the emphasis on aesthetic and intellectual stimulation, the cornerstone of this sanctum lies in the principles of comfort and ergonomics. Recognizing that the language acquisition journey is a marathon, not a sprint, the learner's sanctuary must prioritize sustainability over fleeting convenience. Ergonomic furniture, offering support and comfort, becomes the foundation upon which study hours are built, ensuring that the physical vessel remains resilient, free from the strains and aches that could otherwise divert focus. The configuration of this space, from the height

37

of the desk to the lumbar support of the chair, adheres to the principles of human-centered design, acknowledging that the pursuit of knowledge, in its most enduring form, requires a harmonious relationship between mind and body.

In this meticulous orchestration of space, resources, cues, and comfort, the multilingual nook transcends its physical boundaries, becoming a microcosm of the world's linguistic diversity. It is a testament to the learner's commitment, a space where the world's noise fades into the background, leaving only the clarity of focus and the joy of discovery. Amidst the curated calm of this environment, languages cease to be abstract constructs, evolving instead into vibrant bridges connecting the learner to the vast tapestry of human culture and thought. In this haven, designed with intention and nurtured with care, the seeds of multilingualism find fertile ground, promising blooms of understanding that reach beyond words into the heart of shared human experience.

Time Management Strategies for Busy Learners

In the intricate dance of daily life, where countless tasks clamor for attention, the pursuit of multilingual proficiency is often relegated to the shadowy margins of 'someday.' Yet, within this whirlwind of commitments, a systematic approach to time management emerges, not merely as a lifeline but as a catalyst, transforming fleeting moments into bastions of linguistic growth. This deliberate orchestration of priorities, microlearning sessions, routines, and time-blocking techniques unveils a path where the acquisition of languages flourishes, even amidst the tumult of a bustling schedule.

Prioritization

The act of prioritizing language study in the labyrinth of daily responsibilities mirrors the precision of a skilled jeweler who discerns the gems worthy of focus among many stones. This discernment requires a steadfast commitment to one's linguistic aspirations, elevating them from the quagmire of optional pursuits to the echelons of non-negotiable endeavors. It begins with a candid appraisal of one's daily activities, identifying swathes of time consumed by less productive undertakings. Through this lens, the learner reallocates these pockets of time, however small, dedicating them to the nurturing of linguistic prowess. The transformation of idle moments into opportunities for language engagement signifies not just a rearrangement of priorities but a recommitment to the self to cultivate a skill set that transcends the ordinary.

Microlearning Sessions

In the realm of the perpetually busy, the concept of microlearning sessions stands as a beacon of adaptability, offering a bridge between the aspiration for linguistic proficiency and the reality of cramped schedules. These sessions, brief yet potent, integrate seamlessly into the crevices of daily life, from the morning routine to the evening wind-down. Imagine the learner, standing in the queue for morning coffee, flipping through digital flashcards, or the commuter, headphones in ear, absorbing the cadence of a new language through podcasts during the daily transit. These snippets of study, though fleeting, cumulate over time, weaving a rich tapestry of exposure and practice that underpins language acquisition. Microlearning acknowledges time constraints yet refuses to bow to them, championing instead a philosophy of consistency and integration that makes language learning an omnipresent aspect of daily existence.

Routine Building

Establishing a regular, sustainable study routine transcends the mere allocation of time to language learning; it is an act of ritualization, transforming what could be sporadic, aimless engagements into a structured journey toward linguistic mastery. This routine, tailored to fit the unique contours of the learner's lifestyle and commitments, becomes a sanctified part of the day, a period of undisturbed communion with new languages. Whether it is the quiet hours of the morning, the lull of the afternoon, or the solitude of the evening, this carved-out time is guarded, insulated from the world's intrusions. Within this sacred interval, language study evolves from task to tradition, imbued with a sense of purpose and anticipation that fuels the learner's progress. Thus, the routine becomes a cornerstone of the learner's daily life, a steadfast companion on the path to multilingualism.

Time-blocking Techniques

Amidst the ebb and flow of daily commitments, the time-blocking technique emerges as a strategic ally, allowing learners to earmark specific segments of their day for undivided focus on language acquisition. This method, precise in its execution, involves the calendar boundary, where blocks of time are dedicated solely to the pursuit of linguistic fluency. Each block, a bastion against the barrage of distractions, empowers the learner to immerse deeply in study, practice, and reflection. Within these insulated time slots, the learner engages with complex grammatical structures, delves into the nuances of pronunciation, and ventures into the realms of conversation and comprehension. Time-blocking is a declaration of intent, a visible manifestation of the learner's dedication to language learning. It reinforces the sanctity of study time, ensuring that amidst the whirlwind of life's obligations, the quest for multilingual proficiency remains a priority and a protected endeavor.

In the intricate ballet of time management and language learning, these strategies merge to form a coherent approach, where the relentless march of time is not a foe but an ally. The careful prioritization of language study, integrating microlearning sessions into the crevices of daily life, establishing a sacrosanct routine, and strategically deploying time-blocking techniques together weave a fabric of opportunity, resilience, and progress. Within this framework, the busy learner navigates the demands of life, not by succumbing to the chaos but by sculpting moments of purposeful engagement with the languages that call to their spirit. This dance, though complex, is rendered not just feasible but fruitful, charting a course through the tumult toward the shores of linguistic mastery.

Selecting Your Languages: Considerations for Simultaneous Learning

In acquiring multiple tongues, selection transcends mere preference, morphing into a strategic endeavor that demands careful contemplation. This decision, pivotal in its implications for the learner's trajectory, requires a nuanced assessment of linguistic landscapes, personal aspirations, and the pragmatic scaffolding that underpins successful language acquisition.

Language Family and Similarity

Navigating the intricate web of language families and their inherent similarities or disparities offers a fascinating lens through which learners gauge their multilingual ambitions. Opting to learn languages within the same family—such as Spanish, Italian, and French within the Romance languages—presents a double-edged sword. On one flank, the shared etiology, grammatical structures, and vocabulary can accelerate comprehension and fluency, creating a ripple effect where mastery in one begets familiarity in others. Yet, this kinship harbors the potential for linguistic entanglement, where words intertwine, and grammatical rules blur, challenging the learner to maintain boundaries between tongues.

Conversely, diving into languages that diverge sharply in phonetics and in script and syntactical construction—such as juxtaposing Mandarin with Russian—invites a diversity of cognitive engagement but demands a higher toll on mental exertion and time. This path, while arduous, polishes the learner's cognitive faculties, sharpening their linguistic acuity and cultural empathy by bridging vastly different modes of expression and thought.

Personal and Professional Relevance

The resonance of a language with one's personal narrative or professional landscape cannot be overstated. For some, the allure of a language is rooted in ancestral whispers, calling them to reforge lost connections or to weave new threads into their familial tapestry. Professional ambitions steer their course for others, drawing them towards languages that promise unlocked doors and new horizons in their career paths. The allure of Mandarin, with its economic and geopolitical significance, or the widespread utility of English in global business contexts, exemplifies how professional considerations might guide the selection process.

This alignment with personal passions or career trajectories imbues the learning process with intrinsic motivation and ensures that each step is a stride toward fulfilling broader life goals. It transforms the endeavor from an academic pursuit

43

into a profoundly integrated aspect of the learner's identity and aspirations, lending every word learned the weight of personal significance or professional advancement.

Resource Availability

The terrain of language learning resources, uneven in its distribution, significantly influences the language selection process. Languages that bask in the global spotlight enjoy many materials—textbooks, online courses, multimedia content, and vibrant communities of learners and native speakers. This abundance facilitates a smoother journey, offering varied paths to suit different learning styles and preferences.

In contrast, venturing into less-trodden linguistic paths— those of endangered or less commonly taught languages— presents a unique set of challenges. Resources, scarce and often scattered, demand a higher degree of resourcefulness and dedication from the learner. Yet, this scarcity is not without its rewards. It offers the intrepid explorer the chance to become a guardian of linguistic diversity, contributing to the preservation and revival of languages teetering on the brink of oblivion.

Therefore, the pragmatics of resource availability play a crucial role in shaping the learner's journey, dictating not only the pace of progress but also the depth of cultural immersion and understanding achievable.

Challenge Level

In the calculus of language selection, the variable of challenge level looms large, casting long shadows over aspirations and anticipated outcomes. In their complexity, languages do not stand as equals; some, with their familiar alphabets and cognate-laden vocabularies, extend a warm invitation to the learner. With their labyrinthine grammatical structures, tonal intricacies, or unfamiliar scripts, others demand a higher toll in mental fortitude and temporal investment.

This disparity in difficulty levels necessitates a realistic appraisal of one's capacity for sustained effort and the resilience to navigate the inevitable plateaus and troughs of language learning. Opting for languages that align with one's threshold for challenge maximizes the likelihood of persistence and eventual mastery, ensuring that the arduous journey remains within the bounds of achievable endeavor.

In weighing these considerations—linguistic kinship versus diversity, personal resonance versus professional utility, the abundance of resources versus the scarcity, and the spectrum of challenge levels—the learner stands at a crossroads. Each path, with its unique contours and vistas, promises a journey with discoveries and transformations. The act of selection, therefore, is not merely a preliminary step but a foundational one, setting the course for an odyssey that weaves through the tapestry of human language and culture, enriching the learner's mind and soul with every step taken on this intricate, mesmerizing path.

Tools of the Trade: Essential Resources for Multilingual Learners

In the arsenal of the aspiring polyglot, a diverse array of instruments awaits, each with its unique capacity to facilitate the intricate dance of language acquisition. This collection, ranging from the digital avant-garde to the tactile traditionality of paper and ink, constitutes a vital palette for learners to draw in, painting their multilingual narratives.

Digital Apps and Platforms

In the digital domain, applications, and platforms emerge as beacons of innovation, guiding learners through the labyrinth of linguistic intricacies with unprecedented accessibility. These tools, engineered with the precision of linguists and the insight of educators, offer a spectrum of functionalities designed to cater to the multifaceted needs of language learners. Exploring this digital realm reveals applications adept at transforming the monolithic task of vocabulary expansion into a game of points and levels, making each new word a conquest in the learner's quest for mastery. Simultaneously, platforms dedicated to grammar and syntax illuminate the rules and patterns of languages with interactive exercises, each response a stroke in the broader picture of linguistic competence. Integrating these applications into a learner's study plan is not merely an addition but a transformation, turning the solitary endeavor of language study into an interactive journey with feedback, encouragement, and measurable progress.

Traditional Resources

Yet, in this age of digital proliferation, the tactile allure of traditional resources remains undiminished, their tangible presence a grounding force in the often fleeting world of language learning. Textbooks, with their structured pathways through the complexities of language, provide a systematic approach, and their pages are a map guiding learners through the territories of grammar, vocabulary, and culture. Workbooks complement this journey, offering spaces for practice and reflection, where the abstract becomes concrete through writing. Flashcards, in their simplicity, wield a formidable power, enabling learners to build a personal lexicon, each card a building block in the tower of language proficiency. Together, these resources form a bastion of tradition in the learner's toolkit, their physicality a reminder of the enduring value of hands-on engagement with the material.

Multimedia Resources

The tapestry of language learning is further enriched by the threads of multimedia resources, weaving through the auditory and visual realms to create a mosaic of cultural and linguistic exposure. Films and music transport learners into the heart of cultures, and their narratives and melodies are a conduit for authentic language exposure. Dialogues and lyrics, replete with colloquialisms and cultural references, offer a window into the soul of a language, its beauty and complexity laid bare. Podcasts, straddling the line between entertainment and education, serve as aural companions in the learner's journey. Their content ranges from language lessons to discussions steeped in the nuances of daily life across cultures. The strategic use of these resources breaks the monotony of study and embeds language learning within the broader context of cultural appreciation and understanding.

Language Exchange and Tandem Learning

At the confluence of technology and tradition lies the realm of language exchange and tandem learning, a space where learners converge, driven by mutual linguistic and cultural exchange aspirations. Platforms dedicated to this form of learning dismantle geographic and linguistic barriers, connecting individuals across the globe in a shared pursuit of knowledge. In this symbiotic arrangement, conversations flow unscripted and dynamic, with each participant being a teacher and student, and their interactions are a dance of give-and-take. This method, grounded in the reciprocity of learning and teaching, transcends the conventional student-teacher dynamic, fostering a sense of community and shared endeavor among learners. It underscores the inherently social nature of language and its power to connect and create bridges between disparate worlds. Through language exchange and tandem learning, the journey towards multilingualism becomes a shared voyage, illuminated by fellow travelers' collective wisdom and camaraderie.

In the quest for multilingual prowess, the tools at the learner's disposal are as diverse as they are vital, each serving a unique role in the intricate ballet of language acquisition. From the interactivity of digital platforms to the structured journey offered by traditional resources, the immersive experiences provided by multimedia, and the communal learning fostered by language exchange, these tools form the pillars upon which successful language learning rests. Together, they offer a holistic approach, catering to individuals' varied preferences and learning styles, ensuring that the path to linguistic mastery, though challenging, is navigated with precision, engagement, and a profound sense of connection to the languages and cultures that enrich our world.

Building a Personalized Learning Schedule: A Flexible Blueprint

In the tapestry of daily existence, weaving a schedule that incorporates language learning demands precision and a profound understanding of one's temporal landscape. This endeavor, far from being a mere logistical exercise, is a delicate balancing act that harmonizes the myriad threads of life's obligations with the vibrant hues of multilingual aspirations. In crafting a personalized learning schedule, the learner navigates the dual demands of availability and ambition, charting a course that is both sustainable and conducive to the flourishing of linguistic skills.

Assessing Availability

The initial stride in this intricate dance involves an honest assessment of the time at one's disposal. This task requires peeling away the superficial layers of busyness to reveal the core of genuine availability. This introspection transcends mere clock-watching, delving instead into the rhythm of one's life, identifying pockets of time that, though seemingly inconsequential in isolation, cumulate into significant opportunities for language immersion. In this scrutiny, one discovers the malleable nature of time and how even the most packed schedules harbor moments that can be molded, with intention, into sanctuaries of learning. This revelation, though simple, is transformative, turning the perceived scarcity of time into a canvas awaiting the learner's brush.

Balanced Language Rotation

With the scaffolding of available time erected, the focus shifts to the orchestration of language rotation, a strategy ensuring that each language in the learner's repertoire receives attention. This rotation, far from being a rigid alternation schedule, is a dynamic process that respects the fluid nature of interest and progress. It acknowledges that the path to multilingualism is cyclical, with each language ebbing and flowing in prominence within the learner's focus. In this ballet of linguistic exchange, the learner becomes a conductor, guiding the symphony of languages in a harmony that fosters growth without allowing any single tongue to languish in neglect. This approach not only maintains the learner's engagement by staving off monotony but also cultivates a balanced proficiency across languages, each benefiting from the reflective glow of the others.

Incorporating Diverse Activities

The palette from which the learner paints their multilingual journey is rich with the colors of reading, writing, speaking, and listening activities, each a distinct shade contributing to the full spectrum of language acquisition. The integration of these diverse activities into the learning schedule is an art in itself, one that demands creativity and foresight. With its quiet introspection, reading offers a sanctuary of comprehension and cultural insight, while writing serves as the canvas where thoughts and vocabulary are woven into the tapestry of communication. Speaking, the most vivid of these colors, demands the courage to step into the arena of interaction, turning abstract knowledge into the living breath of conversation. Listening, with its subtle nuances, tunes the ear to the music of the language, its rhythms, and intonations. Together, these activities form a holistic approach to language learning, complementing the others in a symphony of cognitive and expressive development. In curating a schedule that embraces this diversity, the learner ensures that their linguistic growth is not one-dimensional but a vibrant unfolding of capability and understanding.

Adjustments and Iterations

Yet, no matter how meticulously crafted, the most exquisite schedules are not immune to the vicissitudes of life and learning. Here, the principle of adjustments and iterations becomes paramount, a recognition that the path to multilingualism, like life itself, is subject to change. Regular reviews of the learning schedule, informed by progress and feedback, allow for a responsive adaptation that aligns with the learner's evolving needs and circumstances. This process, iterative in nature, transforms the learning schedule from a static blueprint into a living document that breathes in rhythm with the learner's journey. It acknowledges setbacks not as failures but as waypoints, opportunities for recalibration and growth. Similarly, unexpected leaps in comprehension or shifts in interest prompt a joyful reimagining of the schedule, ensuring that the learner's engagement and progress remain at the forefront of the multilingual voyage.

In crafting a personalized learning schedule, the learner embarks on a journey that transcends the mere acquisition of languages. This endeavor, with its honest assessment of time, balanced rotation of languages, incorporation of diverse activities, and commitment to adjustments and iterations, is a testament to the learner's dedication to learning and living languages. It is a process that, in its complexity and dynamism, mirrors the multifaceted beauty of the languages it seeks to master, each adjustment a stroke of the brush that brings the learner closer to the masterpiece of multilingualism.

The Role of Motivation in Language Learning: Cultivating Your Why

Identifying Intrinsic Motivation

The tapestry of human endeavor is interwoven with threads of motivation, those unseen forces that propel us toward the summits of our aspirations. In language learning, the search for intrinsic motivation—those deeply personal catalysts born not of external accolades but of an inner calling—becomes paramount. This quest for a 'why' that resonates profoundly demands introspection, a dive into the depths of one's desires and dreams. For some, this motivation might crystallize in the allure of connecting with a grandparent in their native dialect, an endeavor that bridges generations and heals historical fissures. For others, it manifests in the thirst for consuming literature in its original form and a desire to taste the unfiltered essence of works that have shaped the contours of cultures. This intrinsic motivation, once unearthed, serves as a lodestar, guiding the learner through the ebbs and flows of their linguistic journey, transforming obstacles into stepping stones, and imbuing the process with a sense of purpose that transcends mere acquisition of skill.

Overcoming Plateaus with Purpose

Much like mountain climbing, the path to multilingual mastery is fraught with plateaus, stretches where progress seems to stagnate, and the peak fades into the mists of doubt. In the shadow of frustration, the power of a well-cultivated 'why' reveals itself, transforming from a quiet whisper into a clarion call that rekindles the flames of determination. This intrinsic motivation becomes a rampart against the siege of stagnation, reminding learners of the deeper purpose that set them on this path. It whispers of ancestral connections waiting to be rekindled, literary worlds awaiting exploration, and self-transformation that lies just beyond the horizon of perseverance.

Armed with this purpose, learners find the strength to push against the inertia of plateaus, to innovate in their strategies, and to rekindle the joy of discovery that first set their hearts alight. The plateau, rather than a sign of failure, becomes a rite of passage, a test of resolve that, once overcome, fortifies the traveler's spirit for the journey ahead.

Celebrating Milestones

In the chronicle of language acquisition, milestones serve as beacons, illuminating the path traversed and fueling the journey forward. Recognizing and celebrating these milestones— mastering a complex grammatical structure, conversing with a native speaker, or understanding a film without subtitles— becomes a ritual of affirmation, a tangible acknowledgment of progress that nourishes the learner's motivation. These celebrations, whether through a solitary moment of reflection or shared joy with fellow travelers, serve as reminders of the journey's worth, of the incremental victories that weave together to form the tapestry of mastery. They remind the learner that every step forward, no matter how small, is a triumph over the inertia of the status quo, a testament to their dedication and growth. In this celebration of milestones, motivation finds renewal, transforming the daunting expanse of the journey ahead into a series of attainable vistas, each awaiting the mark of the traveler's footprints.

Community and Social Support

Though embarked upon by the individual, the odyssey of language learning flourishes within the embrace of community. The support, encouragement, and accountability afforded by fellow travelers transform the journey from a solitary endeavor into a shared adventure. Engaging with language learning communities, whether through online platforms, local meetups, or tandem partnerships, weaves a safety net of solidarity, wherein each member finds strength in the collective pursuit of linguistic prowess.

This camaraderie becomes a wellspring of motivation, where the successes of one inspire all, and the challenges faced by any become battles fought by the community. In this confluence of aspirations and endeavors, learners find the encouragement needed to persevere through the troughs of their journey and the joy of contributing to the success of others. In its collective wisdom and diversity, the community becomes a mirror reflecting the multifaceted beauty of language learning, reminding each member of the larger purpose that unites them. In this shared space, motivation is not a finite resource but a renewable energy generated by collective passion and nurtured by the bonds of shared endeavor.

In the dynamic interplay of intrinsic motivation, the overcoming of plateaus, the celebration of milestones, and the support of the community, the learner navigates the complex landscape of language acquisition. Each element, in its unique capacity, contributes to the cultivation of a resilient and renewable motivation capable of weathering the storms of doubt and inertia. This motivation, rooted in the depths of personal aspiration and nurtured by the camaraderie of fellow travelers, becomes the driving force behind the learner's journey, transforming the daunting pursuit of multilingualism into an adventure marked by growth, discovery, and connection.

Overcoming the Initial Hurdles: Practical Tips for Getting Started

In the nascent stages of acquiring new languages, many barriers loom, their daunting silhouettes casting long shadows over fledgling aspirations. These initial obstacles, from the paralysis of perfectionism to the dissonance of unrealistic expectations, require both acknowledgment and strategic circumvention. The following insights aim to equip you with pragmatic approaches to dismantle these barriers, thus paving a path toward linguistic dexterity unfettered by the inertia of commencement.

Action Over Perfection

With its insidious grip, the specter of perfectionism often ensnares learners in a web of procrastination, their endeavors stifled by the fear of missteps. The antidote to this paralysis lies not in the eradication of error but in its embrace, acknowledging that missteps are not the antithesis of progress but its companions. The resolve to act, to utter imperfect phrases and grapple with unfamiliar syntax, becomes a declaration of defiance against the tyranny of perfectionism. This resolve, fortified by the understanding that proficiency is forged in the crucible of consistent effort rather than in the avoidance of error, transforms the initial foray into language learning from a pursuit of flawlessness into an exploration of growth and discovery.

Simple Language Exchanges

Engagement in language exchanges, those reciprocal conduits of learning, presents an invaluable opportunity for practical skill enhancement. In the embryonic stages of language acquisition, the allure of complex dialogues may beckon, yet the wisdom of simplicity prevails. Initiating exchanges with rudimentary greetings, inquiries about the day, or expressions of likes and dislikes lays a foundation for confidence. These simple exchanges, though modest in their linguistic complexity, serve as vital arenas for applying developing vocabulary and grammar, their iterative nature reinforcing learning through repetition and variation. Moreover, the reciprocal aspect of these exchanges imbues them with a sense of contribution, the knowledge that while honing your skills, you are simultaneously facilitating another's journey, thus fostering a sense of community and shared purpose.

Setting Realistic Expectations

The landscape of language learning is often romanticized, its challenges understated in the glow of idealized outcomes. This misalignment between expectation and reality becomes a fertile ground for disillusionment, where the inevitable confrontations with difficulty breed a sense of discouragement. Cultivating realistic expectations, therefore, emerges as a critical endeavor, an act of calibration that aligns aspirations with the pragmatic contours of the learning process. Recognizing that fluency is not the product of weeks but of months or even years of dedicated effort mitigates the sting of setbacks, framing them not as failures but as integral facets of the learning curve. This recalibration of expectations, grounded in the realities of language acquisition, nurtures resilience, enabling learners to navigate the vicissitudes of their journey with poise and persistence.

Resource Exploration

The odyssey towards multilingualism is replete with many tools, each offering unique pathways to linguistic prowess. Yet, amidst this abundance, the challenge of selection emerges, a quest to identify those resources that resonate with one's learning style and objectives. The encouragement to experiment and dabble in various methods and materials becomes a clarion call to action. This exploration, characterized by trial and adaptation, allows learners to curate a personalized toolkit that harmonizes with their preferences, challenges, and aspirations. Whether it be the interactive allure of digital applications, the structured journey offered by traditional textbooks, or the immersive experience of multimedia resources, this process of exploration and selection ensures that the learner's arsenal is diverse and tailored, equipped to address the multifaceted dimensions of language learning.

In the crucible of the beginning, where the raw elements of aspiration meet the heat of effort, the strategies of acting over awaiting perfection, engaging in simple language exchanges, setting realistic expectations, and exploring diverse resources serve as the alchemical processes by which the base metal of initial endeavors is transmuted into the gold of linguistic fluency. These practical insights, far from mere tactics, are the manifestations of an ethos that values progress over perfection, engagement over accuracy, and adaptation over rigidity. They embody the understanding that the journey of language learning, with its peaks and troughs, is not a testament to the learner's initial proficiency but to their resilience, curiosity, and relentless pursuit of growth.

As we transition from the foundational strategies outlined in this chapter, we carry forward the principles of action, engagement, realism, and exploration. These principles, woven into the very fabric of our approach to language learning, prepare us to navigate the complexities of advanced linguistic acquisition and cultural immersion with a mindset attuned to the challenges and joys of multilingual exploration. In this spirit of preparedness and adaptability, we look ahead, ready to delve deeper into the intricacies of mastering multiple languages, armed with the knowledge that every hurdle surmounted enriches our journey, and every barrier overcome brings us one step closer to the boundless horizons of linguistic and cultural mastery.

Chapter 3: Weaving Languages into Your Cognitive Tapestry

Imagine standing before a loom, threads of varied hues at your fingertips, each representing a different language waiting to be interwoven into the fabric of your mind. Weaving these threads of integrating multiple languages into a coherent cognitive tapestry demands techniques as deliberate and nuanced as those of a skilled weaver. Among these techniques, interleaving practice emerges as a pivotal strategy, akin to the art of choosing when and how to blend these threads to create a pattern that is both intricate and robust.

Interleaving, a method where subjects or skills are mixed or interleaved during practice, contrasts with blocked practice, where one skill is repeated before moving on to another. Picture a chef who alternates between chopping vegetables, simmering sauces, and sautéing meats rather than completing each task in isolation. This chef, through interleaving, becomes adept at the dance of cooking, their mind and body syncing in a rhythm that fluidly transitions from one task to the next.

Similarly, when learning languages, interleaving enables the brain to make swift and seamless switches, enhancing both flexibility and retention.

Interleaving Practice: The Secret to Mastering Multiple Languages

Cognitive Flexibility

Interleaving fosters cognitive flexibility, training the brain to pivot quickly between different languages. It's akin to a musician who plays multiple instruments within a single composition, their mind agile, adapting to the unique demands of each instrument without pause. This agility is paramount in a world where switching between languages is often spontaneous and contextual. By mirroring these real-world demands in practice, interleaving prepares the mind for the fluidity required for multilingual communication.

Enhanced Retention

Research underscores the efficacy of interleaved practice in bolstering long-term retention. A study by Rohrer and Taylor at the University of South Florida found that students who used interleaving to study mathematics could apply their knowledge to solve novel problems better than those who used blocked practice. In language learning, this translates to an enhanced ability to remember and apply vocabulary, grammar, and cultural nuances across multiple contexts, making each language a living part of the learner's repertoire rather than a static body of knowledge.

Application in Daily Study

Integrating interleaving into daily study routines begins with a deliberate plan. Allocate time slots for each language you're learning, ensuring a mix within each study session rather than dedicating entire days or weeks to a single language. This could mean practicing Spanish verb conjugations, then switching to Mandarin tones, followed by French vocabulary, within a single study period. This approach not only mimics the naturalistic language switching experienced in multilingual environments but also keeps the brain engaged and alert, preventing the complacency often bred by repetition.

Avoiding Interference

A common concern with interleaving practice is linguistic interference, the potential for languages to entangle the learner's mind. To mitigate this, focus on contrasting elements of the languages learned during interleaved sessions. For instance, if Spanish and Italian, both Romance languages, are in your repertoire, alternate studying their distinct grammatical structures or idiomatic expressions rather than similar vocabulary. This conscious divergence helps to classify the languages within the brain, reducing confusion and promoting clarity in recall.

Visual Element: Interleaving Schedule Template

Below is a template for a weekly interleaving schedule to facilitate the application of interleaving in your language learning routine. Customize it to fit the languages you're learning, adapting the duration and frequency based on your availability and learning goals.

Monday:
   - 30 mins Spanish Grammar
   - 30 minutes Mandarin Listening Comprehension
   - 30 mins French Vocabulary

Tuesday:
   - 30 mins Mandarin Tone Practice
   - 30 mins French Grammar
   - 30 mins Spanish Speaking Practice

[Continue for each day of the week]

This template serves as a scaffold, a starting point to build a routine that aligns with your unique learning journey. The goal is not rigid adherence but flexible adaptation, allowing for adjustments as you discover what combinations and sequences of language study yield the best results for you.

In weaving languages into your cognitive tapestry through interleaving practice, you embark on a path that is both scientifically grounded and enriched by the nuanced beauty of multilingualism. This technique, emphasizing flexibility, retention, and strategic application, equips you to navigate the complexities of learning multiple languages gracefully and effectively. It transforms the challenge of juggling languages from a daunting endeavor into an achievable, enriching pursuit that celebrates multilingual mastery's cognitive and cultural richness.

The Spaced Repetition System: Maximizing Memory Retention

In cognitive science, the theory behind spaced repetition unfurls as a beacon, illuminating the path toward enduring memory retention. This method, underpinned by the forgetting curve hypothesized by Hermann Ebbinghaus, suggests that information is lost over time when there is no attempt to retain it. Spaced repetition, then, acts as the antidote to this natural decay of memory, employing increasing intervals of time between reviews of learned material to cement it into long-term memory. This technique leverages the psychological spacing effect, ensuring that each encounter with the material occurs just as it begins to fade from memory, strengthening the mental retrieval paths with each review.

Applying the Spaced Repetition System (SRS) in language study transforms the daunting task of memorizing vast lexicons and complex grammatical rules into a manageable process. SRS tools and applications, designed with algorithms to adjust review schedules based on individual performance, offer a tailored approach to language learning. These digital companions prompt learners to review words or concepts before they are predicted to forget them, thus optimizing the repetition timing for maximum memory retention. For the language learner, this translates to engaging with an app where each flashcard swipe tests their recall and smartly calculates when they'll next need to revisit the material to aid their learning curve best.

Customization for multiple languages within SRS schedules demands a nuanced strategy, ensuring balanced exposure across the linguistic spectrum the learner aims to conquer. This involves the allocation of dedicated time slots for each language within the SRS tool and a thoughtful consideration of the learner's proficiency and goals in each language. Tailoring the SRS schedule might mean more frequent reviews for a newly introduced language or focusing on complex grammar points for a language in which the learner seeks advanced proficiency. This personalization ensures that every minute spent in review is effectively targeted, fostering growth across all languages in the learner's repertoire without overwhelming them or allowing any one language to dominate their study time.

Yet, spaced repetition extends beyond mere vocabulary acquisition; it is equally potent when applied to grammar rules and language structures. This broader application involves creating custom flashcards that encapsulate vital grammatical concepts, example sentences that illustrate these concepts in action, and structured exercises that challenge learners to apply these rules creatively. By scheduling these grammar-focused reviews in spaced intervals, learners solidify their understanding and ability to manipulate complex language structures, moving beyond rote memorization to a more profound mastery that supports fluent expression and comprehension.

A multitude of resources stand ready to assist the learner in navigating the intricacies of applying SRS to language learning. From specialized SRS applications tailored for language study to customizable flashcard systems that permit the integration of multimedia elements, the options are vast. These tools facilitate and enrich the spaced repetition process, allowing learners to incorporate images, audio clips, and even video snippets into their study materials. This multimodal approach caters to varied learning preferences and reinforces memory through multiple sensory pathways.

Moreover, the journey through spaced repetition is one of continuous adaptation. As learners progress, their review schedules need regular refinement based on performance analytics provided by SRS tools. This data-driven approach ensures that the spacing of reviews remains optimally challenging, both sparse to allow forgetting and too frequent to waste effort on material already mastered. The beauty of SRS lies in its flexibility; it evolves with the learner, constantly fine-tuning the balance between challenge and review to foster productive learning.

As the learner progresses through their multilingual journey, the Spaced Repetition System stands as a steadfast ally, a systematic approach that transforms the ephemeral into the enduring. This technique, grounded in the science of memory and tailored through technology, offers a structured yet flexible pathway to language mastery. It ensures that every word, every grammatical nuance, and every structural complexity is not merely encountered but woven into the fabric of the learner's cognitive landscape, ready to be retrieved and used with confidence. Through spaced repetition, the languages that the learner seeks to master do not remain distant goals but become integral parts of their expressive and interpretive toolkit, available for spontaneous recall and use in the rich tapestry of multilingual communication.

Contextual Learning: Harnessing the Power of Real-world Application

In acquiring languages, the integration of real-world relevance must be balanced. This method breathes life into the skeleton of grammatical rules and vocabulary lists, clothing them in the rich fabric of everyday use and cultural nuance. The significance of this approach lies in its capacity to transform abstract knowledge into a tool for authentic communication. In essence, it shifts the focus from learning about the language to living through the language. When learners encounter new words or grammatical structures in real-life situations, these elements are imbued with meaning, making them easier to remember and apply. This process mirrors how children learn their first language, absorbing the sounds and structures through daily interactions long before they encounter the formal study of grammar.

The inclusion of cultural immersion deepens this contextual learning, acting as a catalyst that accelerates the comprehension and retention of the language. It provides a critical layer of understanding that transcends the mere ability to construct grammatically correct sentences, enabling learners to grasp the subtleties of meaning that can only be understood through cultural context. For instance, idiomatic expressions, which often defy direct translation, become accessible when learners experience them within the cultural situations they naturally arise from. This immersion into the cultural underpinnings of a language fosters a more intuitive grasp, where learners begin to think in the target language rather than translating from their native tongue.

Practical activities offer a tangible means to incorporate this contextual learning into home and community environments. Cooking recipes in the target language can be a multifaceted learning activity at home. Not only does this task require comprehension of the language regarding ingredients and cooking techniques, but it also introduces learners to the cultural significance of certain dishes and their role in the target culture's daily life. Attending cultural festivals or participating in language meetups in the community can immerse learners in a rich tapestry of linguistic practice and cultural exchange. Such experiences reinforce language skills and deepen cultural appreciation, making the language a living part of the learner's world.

69

Simulating scenarios play a pivotal role in contextual learning, especially for those who might not have immediate access to immersive cultural experiences. This involves creating realistic language use scenarios within a controlled learning environment. For instance, role-playing exercises can simulate a market transaction, a job interview, or a doctor's visit in the target language. These simulations can be enhanced with props, multimedia resources, and even participation from native speakers to add authenticity. By acting out these scenarios, learners apply their language skills in a dynamic, pressure-free setting, preparing them for real-world interactions. This practice boosts linguistic confidence and equips learners with the cultural knowledge necessary to navigate similar situations outside the classroom.

In harnessing the power of real-world application through contextual learning, the traditional boundaries of language education dissolve. This approach recognizes that languages are not merely academic subjects to be mastered but are vibrant expressions of culture meant to be experienced and lived. It acknowledges that true linguistic proficiency comes not from the ability to pass a test but from the capacity to engage with the world in another language. Through integrating cultural immersion, practical activities, and the simulation of real-life scenarios, learners are not just studying a language; they are stepping into a new way of seeing, understanding, and interacting with the world. This transformation marks the transition from language learner to language liver, a shift that opens doors to new experiences, perspectives, and connections.

Comparative Linguistic Analysis: Cross-language Insights

In the nuanced field of multilingual studies, comparative linguistic analysis stands as a beacon, guiding learners through the intricate web of languages they aspire to conquer. This process, akin to mapping the DNA of languages, unveils patterns and connections that, once recognized, can dramatically streamline the learning process. By dissecting languages to their core—identifying their grammatical blueprints and lexical threads—learners craft a scaffold upon which multiple languages can coexist, each supporting the others in a harmonious structure.

Identifying Patterns

The quest to uncover patterns across languages is not merely an academic exercise but a practical strategy that can unlock accelerated learning pathways. This endeavor requires a discerning eye, one capable of sifting through the surface differences to uncover the underlying syntactical and lexical frameworks that many languages share. For instance, discovering common Indo-European roots presents a goldmine for learners navigating languages within this family, revealing shared vocabulary and evolutionary grammatical structures. Such insights empower learners to transfer knowledge from one language to another, turning learning a new language into an exercise of connecting dots

71

along a familiar path rather than charting unknown territory. Techniques to facilitate this pattern recognition include comparative charts that juxtapose verb conjugations, noun declensions, or sentence structures across languages, providing a visual matrix of similarities and divergences.

Transferable Skills

The concept of transferable skills lies at the heart of comparative linguistic analysis, embodying the idea that mastery in one language can catalyze proficiency in another. This principle extends beyond the shared vocabulary or Grammar to encompass cognitive and metalinguistic skills honed during the study of one language. For example, navigating the subtleties of aspect and mood in Russian verbs sharpens the learner's grammatical understanding, which proves invaluable when tackling the subjunctive moods of Romance languages. Likewise, developing a keen ear for tonal variations in Mandarin enriches the learner's phonemic awareness, enhancing their capacity to perceive and produce the nuanced vowel lengths and pitches in languages like Thai or Vietnamese. Embracing this concept requires learners to reflect on the skills each language demands, consciously applying these competencies across their linguistic repertoire, thus knitting a tight weave of interconnected knowledge and ability.

Mindful Comparison

While the juxtaposition of languages offers a fertile ground for accelerated learning, it also harbors the potential for confusion, where the lines between languages blur, leading to lexical and grammatical cross-contamination. The antidote to this challenge lies in mindful comparison, a deliberate practice of contrasting languages with an emphasis on their unique features as much as their similarities. This strategy entails a deep dive into the quirks defining each language's character, from idiomatic expressions and cultural references to syntactic constructions with no parallels elsewhere. By anchoring each language in its distinctiveness, learners cultivate mental compartmentalization, linguistic cubism, where each language maintains its integrity even as it interacts with others in the learner's mind. This mindful comparison prevents interference and enriches the learner's appreciation for the diversity and beauty inherent in each language.

Language Learning Synergies

At the zenith of comparative linguistic analysis lies the exploitation of language learning synergies, those points of convergence where learning multiple languages mutually reinforces and amplifies understanding. These synergies manifest in various forms, from the cognitive, where the brain's enhanced neuroplasticity from learning one language boosts the capacity to understand another, to the metacognitive, where strategies for language acquisition are refined and applied more effectively across languages. Further, the cultural insights gleaned from one language illuminate the learner's approach to others, fostering a more profound empathy and connectivity with the languages' native speakers.

To tap into these synergies, learners might engage in thematic studies, exploring a universal concept—such as love, honor, or freedom—across their chosen languages, examining how it is linguistically constructed and culturally contextualized. This holistic approach streamlines the learning process and elevates it, transforming the multilingual endeavor into a rich tapestry of interconnected wisdom that spans languages and cultures.

In traversing the landscape of comparative linguistic analysis, learners wield a powerful toolset: the discernment to identify cross-language patterns, the strategic application of transferable skills, the mindfulness to compare and contrast languages deliberately, and the insight to harness learning synergies. Each of these elements, woven together, forms a robust framework for multilingual mastery, enabling learners to navigate the complexities of multiple languages with precision and grace. This analytical approach, deeply rooted in the recognition of languages as both distinct and interconnected entities, empowers learners to build their linguistic repertoire not as a collection of isolated competencies but as a cohesive, interwoven whole. Through this lens, the study of multiple languages evolves from a daunting challenge into an enriching exploration of the human capacity for communication and understanding, a journey marked by continuous discovery and boundless potential.

The Role of Mnemonics in Multilingual Learning

Within multilingual education, mnemonic devices stand as silent sentinels, guiding learners through the labyrinth of language acquisition with subtle finesse. These tools, deceptively simple in their construct, are potent allies in the battle against forgetfulness, weaving a mesh of memory that holds fast to the myriad details of languages. The essence of mnemonics lies not merely in rote memorization but in creating vivid, indelible associations that anchor linguistic elements to the learner's cognitive framework, ensuring that words, grammar rules, and phrases are not just learned but ingrained.

The landscape of mnemonic techniques is as varied as it is vast, ranging from using acronyms and visual imagery to crafting elaborate narratives that embed language elements within the fabric of memorable stories. Each method serves a distinct purpose, tailored to the distinctive nature of the information it seeks to encode. Acronyms, for instance, can condense lists or sequences into manageable, easily recalled chunks. The acronym ROYGBIV, representing the colors of the rainbow, exemplifies this technique's efficacy. Applied to language learning, similar acronyms can simplify complex grammatical sequences or categorize cohesive vocabulary groups, providing learners with mental shortcuts that facilitate recall.

Diving deeper into the mnemonic arsenal, visual imagery

emerges as a powerful tool, especially in vocabulary acquisition. This technique leverages the brain's inherent propensity for visual processing, transforming abstract words into concrete images that capture the essence of their meaning. A learner might visualize a 'cat' wearing a 'hat' to remember the Spanish word 'gato,' linking the familiar image to the foreign term through rhyme and visual unity. This method not only aids in recall but also adds an element of fun to the learning process, making the retention of new vocabulary an exercise in creativity.

The construction of personalized mnemonics for languages elevates this technique from a mere memorization strategy to a deeply individualized learning experience. Here, learners are encouraged to forge their associations, drawing on personal experiences, interests, or humor to create mnemonics that resonate on a personal level. The effectiveness of this approach lies in its customization; by leveraging individual memory anchors, these mnemonics become uniquely memorable to the creator, ensuring that the language elements they encode are readily accessible.

Cross-language mnemonics represent a refined application of this technique, designed specifically for the multilingual learner. This approach exploits the interconnected nature of languages, using knowledge from one language to facilitate learning in another. For example, a learner fluent in Spanish might use the similarity between the Spanish word 'sopa' (soup) and the French' soup' to create a mnemonic that links the two, reinforcing memory across languages. This method not only streamlines vocabulary acquisition but also highlights the shared linguistic heritage of languages, offering insights into their evolution and connections.

Amidst the array of mnemonic strategies, the method of loci, or the creation of memory palaces, stands as a testament to the technique's ancient roots and enduring utility. This method invites learners to construct mental towers, rooms, or palaces wherein each nook and cranny serves as a repository for language information. By mentally 'walking' through these spaces, learners can visually encounter and recall the linguistic elements stored within. For multilingual learners, each room or wing of the palace might be dedicated to a different language, with specific locations within each space reserved for vocabulary, grammar, or phrases. The spatial organization of the memory palace mirrors the structural organization required for language mastery, providing a mental framework that supports the segregation and retrieval of multiple languages.

The employment of mnemonics in multilingual learning, from crafting vivid visual imagery to constructing elaborate mnemonic palaces, represents a confluence of art and science. It acknowledges the complexity of language acquisition and the challenges inherent in learning multiple languages simultaneously, offering practical and adaptable tools. In their diversity and flexibility, these mnemonic techniques cater to individuals' unique needs and learning styles, providing a personalized approach to language learning that is both engaging and productive.

In the realm of mnemonics, the journey of language learning transcends the mere accumulation of knowledge, transforming into an exploration of the mind's capacity to create, store, and retrieve information. Through the deliberate application of mnemonic devices, learners enhance their ability to remember linguistic elements and deepen their engagement with the languages they seek to master. This engagement, rooted in personalization and creativity, ensures that the languages learned are not fleeting acquaintances but lifelong companions woven into the learner's cognitive tapestry.

Incorporating Multisensory Learning for Deeper Comprehension

The tapestry of language acquisition, rich in its complexity, invites exploration into the realm of multisensory learning, where the engagement of multiple senses enriches the process and anchors the language more firmly in the learner's mind. This approach, embracing the full spectrum of sensory experience, transcends traditional auditory and visual methods, delving into tactile and kinesthetic dimensions to unlock a more profound level of comprehension and retention. In this intricate dance of senses, the learner becomes not merely a receptor of linguistic input but an active participant in a dynamic, immersive learning experience.

The advantages of a multisensory approach lie in its alignment with the brain's natural inclination for holistic processing. Information received through multiple channels creates a web of associations, making retrieval more efficient and learning more durable. This method mirrors how languages are experienced in natural settings, where words are not isolated sounds or symbols but elements of a vibrant, multisensory reality. Engaging the senses in tandem, therefore, simulates real-life language use and taps into the brain's innate capacity for sensory integration, enhancing the depth and breadth of language acquisition.

Tactile Learning Activities

In the tactile dimension, the hands become a conduit for linguistic exploration, transforming abstract concepts into tangible experiences. Consider the act of writing, where the physical movement of a pen on paper can reinforce memory through muscle memory and the tactile sensation of the writing process. Expanding further, the assembly of language puzzles is an innovative exercise where learners piece together sentences or match words with their meanings, engaging both the mind and the hands. This tactile engagement, especially with visual cues, solidifies language connections, embedding them more deeply in the learner's cognitive framework. Activities such as these diversify the learning experience and cater to tactile learners, for whom physical interaction with material is a key to unlocking comprehension.

Visual and Auditory Integration

Integrating visual and auditory materials is a testament to the synergistic power of combining senses in language learning. This method, leveraging the potent duo of sight and sound, mirrors the natural acquisition of language, where visual context and auditory input converge to create meaning. Incorporating films, videos, or even illustrated audio books into the learning repertoire allows learners to experience language in a context-rich format, where the visual narrative enhances understanding and retention of auditory information. Subtitled films, in particular, offer a unique opportunity for learners to match spoken words with their written forms, engaging both the aural and visual cortexes, thus promoting a more nuanced grasp of pronunciation, intonation, and language structure.

Kinesthetic Learning

For kinesthetic learners who thrive on movement and physical engagement, integrating kinesthetic activities into language learning opens new avenues for comprehension and retention. This might involve physical responses to verbal commands, where actions reinforce understanding, or role-playing scenarios requiring learners to navigate a scrics of physical and linguistic challenges. Such activities break the monotony of stationary study and embed language learning within a framework of movement and action, making it more memorable and engaging. The act of physically moving through a space, whether gesturing during a conversation or walking through a role-play scenario, anchors language in a context of action and interaction, reflecting the dynamic nature of real-world language use.

The multisensory approach to language learning, embracing the tactile, visual, auditory, and kinesthetic, offers a comprehensive strategy that aligns with the brain's natural learning processes. By engaging multiple senses simultaneously, this method ensures that language acquisition is not merely a cognitive exercise but an immersive experience that mirrors the complexity and vibrancy of real-life language use. Through tactile activities that transform abstract words into tangible experiences, the integration of visual and auditory materials that enrich comprehension, and kinesthetic exercises that embed learning in movement, learners are equipped to navigate the nuances of multiple languages with increased efficiency and deeper understanding. In this richly sensory learning environment, languages become not just subjects of study but vibrant, living entities that learners can interact with on multiple levels, promising a more engaging, effective, and enduring language learning experience.

Advanced Note-taking Techniques for Language Learners

In the intricate dance of memorizing and internalizing the nuances of multiple languages, a sophisticated approach to note-taking transforms from a mere auxiliary skill to a central pillar supporting the edifice of linguistic proficiency. This systematic strategy, far beyond the rudimentary jotting down unfamiliar words or phrases, involves a deliberate structuring and organization of language input that caters to both the analytical and creative faculties of the mind. In this structured note-taking, the learner finds a reliable ally, one that not only aids in the retention of newly acquired language elements but also in the active synthesis of linguistic knowledge.

Structured Note-taking

The Cornell system, originally designed to enhance lecture note efficiency, reveals its adaptability and potency when tailored for language study. This method, characterized by dividing the note page into distinct sections for cues, notes, and summary, offers a structured framework that encourages a deeper engagement with the language material. For language learners, this translates to the main note section for new vocabulary, grammar rules, or example sentences encountered during study sessions. On the other hand, the cue column becomes a space for questions that arise during learning or for keywords that trigger the recall of concepts.

The summary at the bottom serves as a concise synthesis of the session's learning, ensuring that the key takeaways are crystallized in the learner's mind. This structured approach facilitates an organized review and encourages critical engagement with the material, prompting questions, connections, and reflections that enrich the learning process.

Visual Organization

With its inherent bias towards visual processing, the human brain finds a natural ally in using visual aids for organizing and retaining information. Mind maps and concept charts emerge as potent tools in this visual strategy, transforming the abstract streams of linguistic input into concrete, visually navigable landscapes. In creating a mind map for a new language concept, the learner begins with a central idea — perhaps a key verb or thematic vocabulary set — and branches out to related words, conjugations, synonyms, or sentences. This radial expansion of ideas not only mirrors the associative processes of the brain but also offers a visual snapshot of linguistic relationships, making complex information more accessible to digest and recall. Concept charts, with their ability to categorize and con- trast information, prove invaluable in comparing grammatical structures or vocabulary across different languages, laying bare the similarities and distinctions that might otherwise remain obscured.

Digital Tools

With its myriad innovations, the digital revolution has yet to leave the note-taking domain untouched. A plethora of digital note-taking applications now offer capabilities far beyond the simple replication of pen and paper, embedding within their frameworks features that cater specifically to the needs of the multilingual learner. These tools, with their ability to incorporate multimedia elements — audio recordings, images, hyperlinks to external resources — enrich the note-taking process, turning static notes into dynamic repositories of language learning. The added functionality of tagging and indexing transforms the organization and retrieval of notes from a cumbersome task into a seamless operation, where specific grammar points, vocabulary themes, or language skills can be accessed with a few clicks. For learners juggling multiple languages, segregating notes into distinct notebooks or folders within these apps ensures that each language's study material remains distinct yet easily integrated into a cohesive learning strategy.

Active Review Systems

The culmination of sophisticated note-taking lies in developing an active review system, a method that elevates the simple re-reading of notes to an engaged interaction with the material. Integrating principles of spaced repetition and active recall, this system prompts regular revisits to the notes, not as a passive observer but as an active participant. Techniques such as creating flashcards from note summaries or practicing rewriting notes from memory reinforce retention and understanding. Incorporating self-testing mechanisms, where learners cover the notes and attempt to recall critical points before checking their accuracy, turns review sessions into opportunities for self-assessment and consolidation of knowledge. This active engagement with the notes ensures that the material studied does not fade into memory oblivion but remains accessible and integrable to the learner's growing linguistic competence.

In navigating through these advanced note-taking techniques, from the structured clarity of the Cornell system to the vibrant visual organization of mind maps, the strategic use of digital tools, and the dynamic engagement of active review systems, the language learner crafts a personalized arsenal. This arsenal, tailored to multilingual study's unique challenges and opportunities, transforms note-taking from a mundane task into a powerful lever for linguistic mastery. Through these methods, the learner captures the fleeting insights and breakthroughs of their study sessions and lays a solid foundation for their linguistic knowledge's continual construction and reconstruction. In this structured yet fluid approach to note-taking, the multilingual learner finds not just a method for managing information but a pathway to deeper comprehension, retention, and active use of the languages that weave through the tapestry of their polyglot ambitions.

Embracing Mistakes: How Errors Enhance Language Acquisition

The shadow of error looms in mastering multiple languages, often seen as a precursor of failure rather than a stepping stone to greater understanding. This profoundly ingrained yet fundamentally flawed perception overlooks the intrinsic value of mistakes as catalysts for cognitive growth and linguistic refinement. The act of erring, far from a mere stumble in the linguistic journey, emerges as a critical component of the learning process, offering unique insights into the mechanics of language and the pathways to mastery.

Learning from Errors

The recalibration of perspective on errors, from obstacles to be avoided to opportunities to be embraced, marks a pivotal shift in the language learning paradigm. This shift acknowledges that each mistake, whether a mispronounced word, a grammatically incorrect sentence, or a misunderstood cultural reference, serves as a beacon, illuminating areas of confusion and gaps in understanding that require further exploration. By analyzing the nature of these errors, learners engage in metacognitive reflection, dissecting their linguistic assumptions and strategies to identify underlying misconceptions or areas for improvement. This reflective process enhances language acquisition by targeting specific areas of weakness. It fosters

86

a mindset of resilience, where a curiosity-driven approach to learning supplants the fear of making mistakes.

Feedback Loops

Establishing feedback loops, channels through which learners receive constructive criticism and guidance in response to their errors, is indispensable in translating mistakes into learning opportunities. These loops, facilitated by interactions with teachers, peers, or language exchange partners, function as mirrors, reflecting the learner's linguistic output through the lens of accuracy and idiomatic usage. The efficacy of feedback loops hinges on their timeliness and specificity, where immediate, focused corrections enable learners to recalibrate their understanding and application of language in real-time. Moreover, these interactions, rooted in a shared commitment to linguistic improvement, cultivate an environment of trust and support, where learners feel empowered to experiment with language and secure that mistakes will be met with guidance rather than criticism.

Risk-taking in Language Practice

The encouragement of calculated risk-taking in language use represents a vital strategy for accelerating language learning and building linguistic confidence. This approach, advocating for the active application of language skills in novel or complex situations, challenges learners to step beyond the comfort of familiar linguistic territory into the dynamic realm of authentic communication. By venturing into conversations, written exchanges, or presentations that stretch their current language abilities, learners expose themselves to the possibility of error. Yet, it is precisely this exposure that drives linguistic growth. When approached with a mindset open to learning from mistakes, risk-taking becomes a powerful engine for advancement, pushing learners to refine their language skills through direct, meaningful engagement with the language in its living context.

Documenting Mistakes

The practice of documenting mistakes and maintaining a record of linguistic errors and the circumstances in which they occurred emerges as a systematic tool for progressive learning. This "mistake journal," far from a ledger of failures, serves as a map, charting the learner's linguistic journey with signposts marking areas of challenge and growth. By regularly reviewing this journal, learners engage in self-assessment, tracking their progress over time and identifying patterns in their errors that may indicate deeper linguistic or conceptual misunderstandings. When paired with reflections on possible causes and strategies for correction, this documentation transforms the journal from a mere record into a strategic tool for targeted improvement. It encourages a proactive stance towards errors, where each documented mistake becomes a puzzle to be solved, a step toward a more profound understanding and mastery of the languages being learned.

A transformation occurs in embracing mistakes as integral to the language learning process. Once feared and avoided, errors become welcomed as signposts of progress, each marking not a setback but an opportunity for growth and deeper understanding. Learners cultivate a resilient, curiosity-driven approach to language acquisition through strategic engagement with mistakes, the establishment of feedback loops, the encouragement of risk-taking, and the systematic documentation of errors. This approach not only accelerates linguistic proficiency but also fosters a mindset of continuous improvement, where the learning journey is propelled not by the avoidance of error but by embracing challenge and the pursuit of mastery.

As we transition from the exploration of embracing mistakes to the broader landscape of language acquisition strategies, the lessons gleaned from our errors resonate as a testament to the adaptive, resilient nature of the learning process. These insights, born from the crucible of mistake and correction, illuminate the path forward, guiding us towards a more nuanced, empathetic, and dynamic engagement with the languages that weave the rich tapestry of human communication.

5

Chapter 4: Cultivating a Multilingual Habitat

Imagine stepping into a garden where each plant, from the sprawling ivy to the vibrant tulips, requires a distinct approach for thriving—some flourish in the sunlight, others in the shade. This garden is akin to the ecosystem of languages within your mind, each with its own needs for nurturing and growth. Therefore, creating a multilingual environment at home becomes akin to gardening, where the right conditions must be meticulously cultivated for each language to bloom.

In this pursuit, transforming your living space into a conducive language habitat is paramount. This endeavor isn't merely about the physical rearrangement of objects or the superficial addition of language-related decor. Still, it involves a deeper, more intentional layering of linguistic and cultural textures that resonate with the essence of each language you're learning.

Creating Your Immersion Environment at Home

Language-Specific Zones

The delineation of language-specific zones within your home serves as a spatial strategy for immersion. This could mean a corner of your living room dedicated to French, where posters of Parisian landmarks adorn the walls, or a study nook for Japanese, lined with shelves of manga and kanji practice books. The key lies in creating distinct physical spaces that segregate and celebrate each language, making the transition from one linguistic zone to another a tactile act of crossing cultural thresholds.

Daily Routines

Integrating target languages into daily routines infuses your day with consistent, natural language exposure. This might involve listening to Spanish podcasts as you prepare breakfast or reviewing Russian vocabulary on flashcards while waiting for your morning coffee to brew. The objective is to weave language learning into the fabric of your daily life, transforming mundane tasks into opportunities for linguistic engagement and making the practice of multiple languages a seamless aspect of your routine.

Decor and Media

The strategic use of decor and media further enriches your immersion environment, turning passive spaces into active language learning hubs. Imagine replacing generic artwork with Italian Renaissance prints or setting a German language film to play in the background. These choices serve as aesthetic enhancements and visual and auditory cues that constantly engage your linguistic faculties, providing immersion that goes beyond conscious study and seeps into the subconscious.

Cultural Elements

Incorporating cultural elements related to your target language deepens your connection and understanding, moving beyond linguistic competence tocultural fluency. This could manifest in the kitchen, where recipes and ingredients for Japanese cuisine invite you to explore not just the language but the culinary traditions of Japan. Or, it might take the form of a mini-library filled with Russian literature, both in original and translated forms, allowing you to immerse yourself in the narratives and idioms that shape the language's expression.

Visual Element: Interactive Language Zone Map

To bring the concept of language-specific zones to life, envision an interactive map of your living space. This map, which could be sketched on paper or designed digitally, highlights each area dedicated to a different language, complete with icons representing the specific cultural and linguistic elements contained within. For the French corner, a miniature Eiffel Tower icon; for the Japanese nook, a sushi roll or manga book. Accompanying this map, a checklist offers suggestions for items and activities to enhance each zone, from language-specific board games to subscription boxes filled with cultural artifacts. This visual and interactive tool not only aids in planning your multilingual habitat but also serves as a dynamic reminder of your commitment to cultivating a diverse linguistic garden.

Transforming your home into a multilingual habitat aims to create an environment where languages thrive not in isolation but in a dynamic interplay, much like the diverse species in a garden. With its zones, routines, decor, and cultural elements, this habitat becomes a living ecosystem where languages grow, interact, and flourish. It reflects a commitment to learning languages and integrating them into the essence of daily life, transforming your living space into a crucible of linguistic and cultural exploration.

Culturing such an environment challenges the traditional boundaries of language learning, proposing a model where immersion is not a distant ideal but a lived reality. It

93

acknowledges that the journey to multilingualism is as much about creating the right conditions for learning as it is about the act of learning itself. In this immersive habitat, every corner turned, every object touched, and every routine followed becomes a thread in the rich tapestry of your linguistic journey, weaving together the sounds, sights, and textures of the languages that speak to your soul.

Virtual Language Exchange: Connecting with Native Speakers Online

In an era where the digital realm transcends geographical barriers, engaging with native speakers through virtual language exchanges has become a pivotal facet of linguistic development. This fusion of technology and traditional language practice offers a dynamic arena where learners can immerse themselves in authentic communication, fostering linguistic prowess and intercultural understanding. The essence of this approach lies in its reciprocity and the genuine connections it cultivates, transforming language learning from a solitary endeavor into a shared voyage of discovery.

Platforms for Exchange

Navigating the vast seas of the internet reveals a plethora of platforms dedicated to facilitating these language exchanges. Each platform's unique set of features caters to diverse preferences and learning objectives. Among these, some stand out for their extensive user bases and sophisticated matching algorithms, connecting learners with partners who share not only language interests but also hobbies and educational goals. Others distinguish themselves through integrated language tools such as built-in dictionaries and correction functionalities, enhancing the efficiency of exchanges. Selecting the right platform involves carefully assessing personal learning styles, desired language combinations, and the functionalities most effectively supporting one's learning journey. A diligent exploration of user reviews and platform policies is also crucial, ensuring a safe and productive environment for language exchange.

Structured Exchanges

The fruitful potential of language exchanges often hinges on the structure and intentionality brought into each session. Without a clear plan, sessions risk devolving into casual chats that, while enjoyable, may not significantly advance language skills. Crafting a framework for exchanges involves setting explicit goals for each session, focusing on conversational fluency, grammatical accuracy, or cultural nuances. This structure might manifest in dedicated time slots for each language, allowing both participants an equal opportunity to practice and learn. Incorporating thematic discussions, role-plays, or specific linguistic challenges can inject variety and depth into sessions, pushing both parties beyond their comfort zones and into zones of proximal development.

Periodic reflection on these sessions, noting progress, challenges, and areas for focus, further refines the process, making each exchange a stepping stone toward linguistic and cultural competence.

Cultural Exchange

The true richness of virtual language exchanges lies in the linguistic practice they afford and the profound cultural insights they unveil. Each conversation becomes a window into another culture's lifestyles, traditions, and perspectives, offering lessons that extend far beyond vocabulary and grammar. For the language learner, these insights are invaluable, providing context that breathes life into the languages being learned and fostering a deep appreciation for the diversity of human experience. Actively seeking out discussions on cuisine, festivals, societal norms, and historical narratives enriches the exchange, transforming it from a mere language lesson into a voyage across cultural landscapes. These exchanges, over time, have the potential to blossom into lasting friendships, offering ongoing support and motivation in the language learning journey.

Consistency and Commitment

The sustainability of virtual language exchanges and their impact on language proficiency is contingent upon the consistency and commitment brought to the process.

Establishing a regular schedule for exchanges provides structure and builds a routine that seamlessly integrates language practice into daily life. This consistency fosters steady progress, with each session building upon the last, gradually enhancing fluency and comprehension. Equally important is the commitment to the exchange relationship, respecting each other's time and efforts, and showing flexibility and understanding for the challenges and obligations that may affect scheduling. Nurturing these relationships with care and mutual respect ensures that language exchanges remain a rewarding and enriching part of the language learning experience, offering continual opportunities for growth and connection in an increasingly interconnected world.

In weaving together these threads of exploration, selection, structured practice, cultural immersion, and dedicated commitment, virtual language exchanges emerge as a vibrant tapestry of linguistic and cultural exchange. They stand as a testament to the power of human connection in breaking down linguistic barriers and offering a pathway to language proficiency, global citizenship, and intercultural empathy. In this digital age, the ability to connect, learn, and grow together, despite physical distances, highlights the boundless possibilities that await within language learning, where every conversation is a bridge to new horizons.

Leveraging Technology for Language Learning: Apps, Podcasts, and More

In the digital age, the landscape of language learning is irrevocably intertwined with technology, offering a plethora of tools that cater to the multifaceted needs of the polyglot. Navigating this landscape requires a discerning approach to selecting the most effective resources, ensuring they simultaneously align with the intricate dance of learning multiple languages.

App Selection

The criteria for choosing apps that support multilingual studies hinge on their flexibility to adapt to varied linguistic landscapes. Look for applications that offer a wide array of languages, facilitating a seamless switch from one language to another within a single interface. This streamlines the learning process and fosters a mental agility conducive to juggling multiple languages. Apps that provide personalized learning paths adapting to your pace and proficiency in each language prove invaluable. They ensure that while you may advance in one language, you won't find yourself plateauing in another. Moreover, consider the depth of cultural insights offered—apps that intertwine language lessons with cultural nuances afford a richer, more contextual understanding, bridging the gap between mere linguistic competence and true cultural fluency.

Podcast Integration

The auditory nature of podcasts renders them a potent tool for immersive language learning, simulating the experience of being enveloped in the linguistic rhythms of native speech. To weave these auditory threads into the fabric of your daily routine, select podcasts that match your proficiency level in each target language, from slow-spoken news for beginners to debate shows for advanced learners. Diversify your playlist to include podcasts exploring cultural themes, history, or stories in your target languages, enhancing listening skills while deepening cultural comprehension. Regularly listening to various accents and dialects within the same language prepares you for the breadth of real-world interactions, fostering an adaptable and nuanced understanding of the spoken word.

Online Communities

The digital realm burgeons with communities where language learners converge, offering mutual support, resources, and the opportunity for practice. These forums, social media groups, and language learning platforms are invaluable for those navigating the complexities of acquiring multiple languages. They offer practical resources—study guides, flashcards, language challenges—and moral support from individuals on similar journeys. By sharing your experiences, challenges, and successes, participating actively in these communities creates a sense of accountability and motivation. Engage in discussions, pose questions, and contribute answers, immersing yourself in a collective learning experience that transcends geographical boundaries and unites learners in their quest for linguistic mastery.

Multimedia Resources

Incorporating a diverse array of multimedia resources into your study regimen addresses the myriad ways individuals engage with and retain new information. Movies and music, for instance, offer more than entertainment; they are conduits for language and culture, embedding vocabulary and expressions within memorable contexts. Watching films in your target languages, with or without subtitles, challenges your comprehension and accustoms your ear to the natural flow of conversation. Similarly, music can be a mnemonic device, with rhythms and rhymes aiding in the retention of tricky phrases or vocabulary. Ebooks, on the other hand, allow for a deeper dive into language structures, offering the chance to see grammar and vocabulary in action. The key is to select resources that interest and challenge you, push your boundaries, and encourage active engagement with the language.

In this digital odyssey of language learning, technology emerges as a tool and a bridge connecting learners to a world of linguistic and cultural richness awaiting exploration. Through careful selection and integration of apps, podcasts, online communities, and multimedia resources, the polyglot navigates this landscape with agility, each step guided by a strategy that marries personal interest with educational value. This approach transforms the solitary act of language learning into an interactive, communal experience enriched by the voices, stories, and songs of cultures around the globe. In leveraging technology in such a multifaceted manner, the learner crafts a personalized, dynamic framework for language acquisition that is both sustainable and joyously enriching.

Language Learning through Media: Movies, Music, and Books

In the intricate dance of absorbing languages, media in its myriad forms plays a pivotal role, not as mere entertainment but as a conduit for immersive learning. This rich tapestry of sounds, visuals, and text beckons with a promise of linguistic enrichment, inviting a deep dive into the cultural soul of languages through selective watching, musical exploration, strategic reading, and the pursuit of artistic wisdom.

Selective Watching

Choosing films and television shows transcends the boundaries of passive viewing into an active engagement with language. This selective screening demands a discerning eye for content that balances enjoyment with educational merit. Imagine scenes where dialogue runs like a river, smooth and uninterrupted—these become arenas for tuning your ear to the natural cadences and colloquialisms of speech. Opt for productions that mirror everyday life, where the language used is as it's spoken on streets and in homes, offering a lens into the linguistic nuances that textbooks often overlook. Subtitles, in this context, serve dual purposes: when matched with spoken language, they reinforce reading skills; when displayed in your native language, they aid comprehension, allowing you to grasp subtleties and expand your vocabulary. This balancing act between entertainment and learning transforms viewing into an active listening and understanding exercise, embedding language within lived experiences.

Music as a Learning Tool

With its rhythms and melodies, music emerges as a powerful ally in language acquisition, transforming memorizing words and phrases into an enjoyable endeavor. Engage with songs in your target languages, letting the melodies guide you into the heart of the language, where emotion and expression blend seamlessly with vocabulary. The process begins with carefully selecting songs whose lyrics resonate or challenge, followed by a deep dive into these lyrics—dissecting them, understanding their meanings, and singing along. Beyond its joy, this act of vocal mimicry serves as pronunciation practice, where the tongue learns the dance of accents and intonations unique to each language. Compile playlists that span genres and eras, exposing yourself to the linguistic diversity within a single language, from the poetic to the everyday. Let music be both a window into the culture that shapes language and a mirror reflecting the progress of your linguistic journey, marked by the songs you learn to understand and, eventually, sing.

Reading Strategies

Integrating reading into your language learning routine involves more than the passive perusal of text; it is an active exploration of language through the printed word. Begin with materials that match your current level of comprehension, gradually increasing complexity as your confidence grows. Newspapers and online articles, with their concise and topical nature, offer snapshots of contemporary usage and colloquial language, making them excellent starting points. As you advance, delve into books—first those written for children and, eventually, literature that challenges and captivates. Employ active reading techniques: underline new vocabulary, jot down intriguing phrases, and summarize passages to reinforce understanding and retention. This systematic approach to reading transforms it from a solitary act into an interactive dialogue with language, where every page turned is a step deeper into linguistic proficiency.

Cultural Insights

Media, in its essence, is a vessel for cultural narratives, carrying within it the values, beliefs, and historical undercurrents that shape societies. You gain access to these cultural insights through movies, music, and books, enriching your understanding of the language beyond mere words. Films reveal gestures and expressions that carry unspoken meanings; songs echo the emotional cadences of a culture; books open doors to the collective psyche, offering context that grounds language in reality. This pursuit of cultural wisdom through media is not a linear path but a spiral, where each piece of media revisited at different points in your learning journey reveals more profound layers of understanding. In this spiraling journey, language transcends the realm of communication to become a bridge to foreign and familiar worlds, inviting not just comprehension but connection.

In weaving together the threads of selective watching, musical exploration, strategic reading, and the pursuit of cultural wisdom, media becomes more than a tool for language learning— it becomes a tapestry rich with the hues of linguistic diversity and artistic depth. This approach, eschewing passive consumption for active engagement, invites a deeper immersion in the languages you seek to learn, transforming every song heard, every page turned, and every scene watched into a stepping stone toward linguistic fluency and cultural understanding. Through this immersive engagement with media, language learning evolves into a journey of linguistic acquisition and artistic discovery, where each piece of media consumed adds a vibrant thread to the ever-expanding tapestry of your multilingual odyssey.

Speaking from Day One: Overcoming the Fear of Conversation

Speaking a new language introduces a paradox of vulnerability and empowerment. The early stages of language acquisition often evoke a fear of miscommunication, a trepidation rooted in the potential for errors and the social faux pas they might entail. Yet, it is through speaking, this very act of stepping into the unknown, that profound strides in fluency and self-assurance are made. The journey to speaking confidence begins not at a distant milestone of perceived readiness but on day one, embracing imperfect articulation as a necessary component of growth.

Forging this path demands reconceptualizing errors not as failures but as invaluable feedback mechanisms. This mindset shift paves the way for practical speaking activities tailored to infuse daily routines with opportunities for verbal practice. Solo exercises, such as narrating one's actions throughout the day or rehearsing hypothetical conversations, serve as a foundation, building a scaffold of familiarity and ease around the target language. Though devoid of real-time interaction, these solitary practices cultivate an internal dialogue that nurtures linguistic agility.

Expanding this practice to include partners, be they fellow learners or native speakers, introduces the dynamics of live conversation. Here, structured or spontaneous language exchanges offer a rich tapestry of colloquialisms and cultural idioms, breathing life into the structured knowledge acquired through study. The key lies in deliberately selecting topics that ignite curiosity and passion, transforming the exchange into a lively discourse rather than a sterile academic exercise. The incorporation of storytelling, where learners recount personal experiences or fictional tales in the target language, adds depth to the interaction, challenging both speaker and listener to navigate the nuances of narrative and emotion.

The technique of language shadowing emerges as a bridge between solitary practice and interactive conversation. This method involves mimicking spoken language from audio recordings and hones pronunciation and intonation by embedding the rhythms and patterns of native speech into the learner's vocal repertoire. When practiced regularly, shadowing acts as a rehearsal for real-life conversation, equipping learners with the fluidity and confidence to engage in spontaneous dialogue. A deeper, more intuitive grasp of the language is forged in the echo of the spoken word, the attempt to mirror its melody and cadence.

Central to these practices is the confrontation and dismantling of perfectionism, a barrier that stifles expression and impedes linguistic progress. Overcoming this barrier requires a recalibration of expectations, acknowledging that fluency is not born from flawless speech but from the willingness to communicate despite imperfections. Strategies to combat this mindset include setting realistic goals for each conversation and focusing on the ability to convey meaning rather than achieve grammatical perfection. Adopting a playful attitude towards speaking, viewing each interaction as an experiment rather than a test, injects a sense of joy and exploration into the learning process. Moreover, establishing a supportive community through language learning groups or online forums offers reassurance and encouragement, reinforcing the notion that mistakes are a universal, and indeed essential, aspect of language acquisition.

Navigating the journey from hesitant speaker to confident communicator demands courage, persistence, and a strategic approach to practice. The fear of conversation is overcome through the integration of practical speaking activities, the rhythmic dance of language shadowing, and the deliberate effort to silence the inner critic. In this endeavor, regardless of accuracy, each spoken word stands as a testament to the learner's commitment and progress, a step closer to talking and living the language.

Traveling as a Language Learning Tool: Tips and Strategies

Venturing beyond the confines of a familiar environment into the realm where languages live in their natural habitat offers an unrivaled method for absorbing linguistic nuances. This section delves into the intricate process of leveraging travel as a pivotal language acquisition component, emphasizing preparation, immersive experiences, the art of maintaining a travel journal, and the invaluable practice derived from local interactions.

Pre-trip Language Preparation

The anticipation of a journey to lands where your target languages unfold in their day-to-day glory necessitates a detailed pre-trip preparation phase. This pivotal phase sets the stage for a trip where language learning transitions from a structured study session to an organic element of every interaction. Begin with an assessment, a detailed inventory of language skills to pinpoint areas requiring immediate attention—conversational fluency or comprehension. Following this, a focused study plan emerges, targeting these identified areas with resources that simulate the immersive experience awaiting. Consider, for instance, fine-tuning listening skills through podcasts featuring dialects of your destination or enhancing speaking abilities by engaging in online exchanges with natives from the region. This targeted preparation ensures that the language learner is not merely a visitor but a participant, ready to navigate the linguistic landscape confidently upon arrival.

Language Immersion Travel

Choosing a destination for language immersion travel transcends the allure of landscapes or the charm of tourist landmarks; it is about identifying locations where language and culture are intertwined, offering a rich tapestry of learning opportunities. When selecting a destination, consider places off the beaten path where the necessity of language use in daily interactions is encouraged and required.

This might mean opting for a small town over a bustling city or a rural community where English is seldom spoken. Once the destination is set, curating experiences becomes the next step. Engage in activities that foster interaction—cooking classes, local workshops, community events—all avenues where language is crucial to participation. These choices ensure that every moment of the journey becomes a lesson, a real-time practice session underpinned by the authenticity of cultural immersion.

Travel Journals

Maintaining a travel journal in the target language serves multiple purposes; it is both a repository for memories and a reflective space for linguistic growth. This journal becomes the canvas where experiences are painted in words, each entry a composition that blends new vocabulary with personal insights. To enhance this practice, include sections dedicated to daily interactions, new phrases learned, and cultural observations.

Additionally, integrating multimedia elements—ticket stubs, restaurant menus, photographs—transforms the journal into a visual complement to written entries, making the recollection of experiences and language learned vivid and engaging. Documenting the journey in the target language solidifies newly acquired knowledge, embedding it within the framework of personal experiences, making the learning profoundly personal and far more memorable.

Local Interaction

The cornerstone of using travel as a language-learning tool lies in the richness of local interactions. Spontaneous and planned interactions are the crucibles where the language is tested, practiced, and refined. Strategies for engaging in meaningful conversations with locals start with a willingness to step into the vulnerability of making mistakes, approaching each interaction with humility and openness to learn. Simple exchanges, asking for directions, or making small purchases become significant in the target language, each a mini-challenge that builds linguistic resilience. Furthermore, expressing genuine interest in the local way of life invites deeper conversations, offering insights into idiomatic expressions and cultural contexts that textbooks seldom capture.

For those keen on maximizing these interactions, consider carrying a pocket-sized notebook, a tool for jotting down new words or phrases encountered in conversations, making every interaction a learning moment. Beyond the immediate benefits of linguistic practice, these interactions weave the social fabric of the travel experience, creating connections that last beyond the journey and enriching the language learner's understanding of the world.

In traversing the paths laid out by pre-trip preparation, immersive travel choices, the diligent maintenance of a travel journal, and the pursuit of local interactions, travel transcends its traditional boundaries. It becomes more than an escape from the mundane; it transforms into a strategic, deeply enriching component of language learning. This approach to travel, focusing on linguistic immersion and cultural engagement, ensures that every step taken in a foreign land becomes a stride towards linguistic fluency, turning the world into a classroom where lessons are lived, experienced, and cherished.

Hosting Multilingual Gatherings: Learning through Socialization

Bringing together minds eager for linguistic exploration under one roof transforms a simple gathering into a crucible of cultural exchange and linguistic enrichment. These assemblies, informal meetups, dinner parties, or themed events become arenas where language serves as both the medium and the message, fostering an environment ripe for learning and connection. The planning and executing of such events necessitate creativity, a deep understanding of the languages involved, and, most importantly, a keen sense of how social interactions can serve as catalysts for linguistic growth.

Planning Language-themed Events

Orchestrating events that orbit around the gravity of language themes calls for an inventive spirit. Imagine, for instance, a soirée dedicated to the French language, where every element, from the invitations to the decor, whispers of Parisian streets, and the rustic charm of the French countryside.

Guests might find themselves navigating through activities that compel engagement in French, from deciphering clues in a language treasure hunt to participating in a cooking demonstration of classic French dishes, guided entirely in the target language. The key to success lies in the details—ensuring that the theme is not merely decorative but deeply integrated into every aspect of the event, encouraging guests to plunge into the linguistic depths with enthusiasm and curiosity.

Cultural Celebrations

The calendar brims with opportunities to anchor gatherings in the rich soil of cultural festivities, where language learning transcends the confines of structured study to blossom in the vibrant atmosphere of celebration. Aligning events with cultural festivals or holidays related to the target languages not only imbues gatherings with authenticity but also offers attendees a taste of the traditions that shape the language. A Japanese Hanami party, where participants gather under the transient beauty of cherry blossoms to share poetry and stories in Japanese, serves as a poignant example. Such events are meticulously planned to reflect the cultural and linguistic nuances of the celebration and provide a multisensory learning experience, deepening both linguistic competency and artistic appreciation.

Language Exchange Meetups

At its core, the foundation of language learning rests on the exchange of knowledge and experiences between individuals. Initiating or joining language exchange meetups brings this principle to life, creating spaces where learners and native speakers converge to share, learn, and grow. These meetups, structured around conversation tables for different languages, allow participants to rotate, immersing themselves in multiple languages throughout the event. The organization of these gatherings hinges on a balance between structured conversation prompts and the freedom for organic interaction, fostering an environment where learning is intentional and spontaneous. Through regular participation, these meetups evolve into communities, offering sustained support and motivation for members on their multilingual paths.

Social Media and Networking

In the digital age, the tendrils of social media extend into every facet of life, including the realm of language learning and socialization. Leveraging these platforms for the organization and promotion of multilingual gatherings taps into a well-spring of potential attendees, broadening the reach of events beyond immediate social circles. Platforms dedicated to event organization offer tools for managing invitations, RSVPs, and discussions, facilitating the logistical aspects of event planning. Beyond logistics, social media is a vibrant forum for post- event engagement—sharing photos, reflections, and resources discovered during the gathering. This digital extension of the event keeps language learning momentum alive, nurturing the connections formed and the linguistic curiosity ignited among participants.

In the orchestration of multilingual gatherings, from the brainstorming of language-themed events and the celebration of cultural festivals to the cultivation of language exchange meetups and the strategic use of social media, lies an acknowledgment of social interaction's profound role in language acquisition. These gatherings, meticulously crafted to merge enjoyment with education, embody the ethos that language learning thrives not in isolation but in the rich soil of community and shared experience. Through these social crucibles, language transcends its role as a subject to be studied, weaving itself into the fabric of relationships, cultural understanding, and personal growth. In this way, every gathering becomes a microcosm of the wider world, a space where languages intermingle, cultures converse, and learners find both fluency and friendship and a deeper connection to the global tapestry of human expression.

The Role of Writing in Language Mastery

Within the intricate fabric of language learning, the act of writing weaves its threads with subtle strength, offering pathways not only to memorize but also to internalize the diverse nuances of multiple languages. This process, ranging from the personal reflections of journaling to the communal sharing of blogs and the intimate exchange of letters, encapsulates the essence of linguistic expression, transforming abstract thoughts into concrete text.

Journaling in Multiple Languages

The habit of journaling, when practiced across the languages one seeks to absorb, becomes more than a mere exercise in writing—it morphs into a reflective mirror, revealing the contours of one's linguistic progression and the depths of understanding achieved. Each entry, penned in a different tongue, serves as a milestone, marking the journey traversed in multilingualism. This methodical recording not only reinforces new vocabulary and Grammar learned but also invites introspection, encouraging learners to ponder their experiences, challenges overcome, and insights gained through the lens of each language. The bilingual or multilingual journal thus stands as a testament to the evolving relationship between the learner and the languages they embrace, charting a course of personal and profound growth.

Blogging for Language Practice

In the digital age, creating a blog dedicated to one's language learning adventures opens a gateway to a global audience, transforming solitary study into a shared venture. This platform allows for the chronicling of linguistic milestones, the challenges encountered, and the strategies employed to simultaneously navigate the complexities of learning multiple languages. Beyond serving as a digital journal, a blog invites interaction—comments from fellow learners, feedback from native speakers, and discussions with enthusiasts from across the globe. This interactive dimension enriches the learning experience, providing diverse perspectives and invaluable input that refine and enhance linguistic skills. Moreover, composing blog posts in various languages pushes learners to polish their written expression, converting passive vocabulary into active, transferable knowledge. Through blogging, language learners hone their writing skills and weave connections, fostering community in the vast digital expanse.

Letter Exchange Programs

Though seemingly archaic in the fast-paced digital world, the art of letter writing holds a unique charm and utility in language learning. Engaging in letter exchange programs with native speakers offers an intimate venue for practice, where the written word becomes a bridge connecting distant lives and experiences. This form of communication demands thoughtful composition, careful selection of words, and attention to grammatical structures, honing writing skills in a manner that electronic communication often overlooks. Furthermore, the anticipation of receiving a letter, the tactile sensation of holding it in one's hands, and the personal touch imbued within handwritten words add motivation and excitement to the learning process. Letters become keepsakes, physical manifestations of a linguistic journey shared between pen pals, each exchange contributing to a deeper understanding and appreciation of the target language and its cultural context.

Creative Writing

Exploring creative writing in target languages unlocks new vistas of expression, inviting learners to venture beyond the confines of conventional exercises into the realm of imagination and storytelling. This pursuit challenges learners to employ their linguistic repertoire innovatively, crafting narratives, poems, or dialogues that breathe life into the vocabulary and Grammar that form the backbone of their study. Creative writing tests one's ability to convey complex ideas and emotions in another language and is a powerful tool for engagement and retention. With its demands for originality and fluency, the creative process fosters a deeper, more intuitive grasp of the language, transforming learners from students to creators, capable of weaving their thoughts and visions into the fabric of their target languages.

In traversing the multifaceted landscape of writing as a cornerstone of language mastery, learners encounter a rich tapestry of methods—journaling, blogging, letter writing, and creative composition—each offering unique benefits and insights. These practices collectively underscore the transformative power of writing in acquiring multiple languages, bridging the gap between passive knowledge and active proficiency.

117

Through writing, learners solidify their grasp of linguistic structures and forge a deeper, more personal connection with the languages they seek to learn. This connection, rooted in expressing thoughts, experiences, and creativity, elevates language study from a mere academic pursuit to a personal and cultural exploration journey.

As we close this chapter, we recognize that the language learning journey is punctuated not by the destinations reached but by the insights gained and the connections forged along the way. In its various forms, writing serves as both a vehicle and a companion on this journey, enriching our understanding, enhancing our skills, and expanding our horizons. It reminds us that mastery lies not in flawless perfection but in the continuous pursuit of expression, knowledge, and connection. With pens poised and keyboards at the ready, we move forward, ever eager to explore the vast landscapes of language that await us.

6

Chapter 5: Tuning Into the Symphony of Sounds

In a world where the din of daily life often drowns out the subtleties of sound, embarking on the quest to attune our ears and tongues to the nuanced symphony of a new language presents an exhilarating challenge. Like a musician first laying hands on an unfamiliar instrument, the initial discordance is inevitable. Yet, with persistence, what once was racket now transforms into harmony. This metamorphosis begins not on grand stages but in the stillness of practice rooms through meticulous tuning of our phonetic awareness and articulatory agility.

The Phonetic Approach: Mastering Sounds from the Start

Understanding Phonetics

Phonetics, the science of speech sounds, offers a map to navigate the terrain of unfamiliar linguistic landscapes. Familiarizing oneself with the phonetic alphabet of each target language serves as the compass for this journey. It's akin to learning the notes on a piano before attempting to play a melody; without this foundational knowledge, one may hit the right keys occasionally, but the music will lack coherence. By internalizing the International Phonetic Alphabet (IPA), learners unlock the ability to decipher pronunciation guides accurately, turning what might appear as arcane symbols into clear, actionable insights into how sounds are produced.

Articulation Exercises

Shaping sounds from another language with our vocal apparatus involves a delicate choreography of muscles unaccustomed to moving in new ways. Consider, for example; the Spanish rolled "r" sound—which, for many non-native speakers, proves elusive. By engaging in targeted articulation exercises, such as tongue trills and position drills, learners can develop the muscular flexibility necessary to produce such sounds. It's not unlike a dancer learning to isolate and control muscles to execute a fluid movement. When practiced consistently, these exercises gradually recalibrate the muscle memory of the mouth and throat to accommodate the unique demands of another language's phonology.

Minimal Pairs Training

Minimal pairs, sets of words that differ by only a single sound (such as "bat" and "pat" in English), serve as an effective tool for honing phonetic discernment. This method sharpens auditory perception, enabling learners to detect and produce subtle sound differences that can alter meaning. Engaging with minimal pairs involves passive listening and active repetition, challenging the learner to mirror the sounds as precisely as possible. In a classroom setting, this might unfold as a playful quiz, with learners tasked to identify the word spoken from pairs presented. At home, recordings of minimal pairs can be used similarly, turning practice into an interactive game.

Feedback and Correction

The path to phonetic mastery is paved with feedback and adjustment. In the digital age, access to native speakers for pronunciation feedback is unparalleled, whether through language exchange apps or tutoring platforms. Technology offers innovative solutions, such as pronunciation apps that use speech recognition to provide instantaneous corrective feedback. Yet, the value of human interaction cannot be overstated. A native speaker can offer nuanced feedback that technology may overlook, such as the appropriateness of a specific pronunciation in a given context or the emotional connotations of a particular intonation. Rather than viewing correction as a critique, embracing it as a gift allows learners

121

to refine their phonetic accuracy with gratitude.

Visual Element: Interactive Phonetics Workbook

A digital or printable workbook designed to accompany this chapter could be an invaluable tool for learners. This workbook could include the following:

• Phonetic Alphabet Charts: These are visual representations of the phonetic alphabet for each target language, coupled
with audio clips for each sound.
• Articulation Exercise Guides: Step-by-step instructions and illustrations for exercises designed to improve mouth and tongue flexibility.
• Minimal Pairs Lists and Audio Quizzes: Curated lists of minimal pairs, along with interactive audio quizzes that test the learner's ability to distinguish and reproduce these
sounds.
• Feedback Logs: Templates for tracking feedback from native speakers or apps, allowing learners to note areas for
improvement and monitor their progress over time.

This workbook, rich with resources and interactive elements, would reinforce the concepts discussed in this chapter and provide learners with a structured framework for practice and self-assessment.

Listening Skills: Strategies for Understanding Native Speakers

The quest to attune our auditory faculties to the musicality of a foreign language demands more than mere exposure to its sounds. It requires a deliberate, systematic approach to dissecting and digesting the nuances of speech that native speakers effortlessly weave into their daily dialogue. The endeavor to refine our listening capabilities unfolds across several fronts, each addressing a distinct aspect of auditory comprehension that, when combined, contributes to a holistic enhancement of our ability to process and understand spoken language in its natural, unfiltered form.

Active Listening Exercises

Engaging the mind in active listening exercises transforms passive hearing into an active decoding process, where every sound, intonation, and pause becomes a piece of a puzzle waiting to be solved. This practice involves more than just absorbing the content of what is being said; it's about dissecting the flow of speech, identifying patterns, and anticipating what comes next—tools for this exercise range from simple, everyday interactions to structured audio materials designed for linguistic training. One might listen to a dialogue or a monologue and attempt to map out the conversation, predicting responses and noting any unexpected deviations. This practice sharpens the ability to

123

comprehend spoken language and enhances predictive linguistic skills, making real-time conversations less daunting and more navigable.

Transcription Practice

The meticulous act of transcribing spoken language bridges listening and writing, reinforcing comprehension through conversion from audio to text. This exercise demands an acute focus, as it challenges the listener to capture the words and the rhythm, pauses, and subtleties that punctuate speech. Learners immerse themselves in the language by transcribing dialogues, interviews, or speeches, paying attention to details that might otherwise slip unnoticed. This practice does not require perfection but rather a dedication to capturing the essence of what is being said, making it an invaluable tool for honing listening skills and attention to detail.

Varied Accent Exposure

Diving into the diversity of accents and dialects within a language opens up a world of phonetic richness, offering listeners a spectrum of vocal expressions to explore. Each accent, with its unique cadence and pronunciation, presents challenges and learning opportunities. By intentionally exposing oneself to various accents, learners can broaden their auditory comprehension and prepare themselves for the multifaceted reality of language as it exists in the world.

This can be achieved through curated playlists of speakers from different regions or by consuming media—films, podcasts, radio shows—that showcase dialectal diversity. Through repeated exposure, these accents' initially unfamiliar sounds and rhythms become less foreign, enhancing the listener's ability to understand and engage with speakers from various linguistic backgrounds.

Contextual Listening

To truly grasp the essence of spoken language, one must delve beyond the words and phrases to the context in which they are embedded. Contextual listening involves understanding the semantics of speech and the situational, cultural, and emotional layers that influence how messages are conveyed and received. This form of listening can be practiced by engaging with audio content rich in artistic and situational context—stories, interviews, and real-life conversations that require the listener to interpret meaning not only from the language used but from the context in which it is used. By focusing on the interplay between language and context, learners can develop a deeper, more nuanced understanding of how meaning is constructed and communicated, paving the way for more meaningful and informed interactions in the target language.

In the pursuit of auditory mastery, these strategies converge to create a comprehensive framework for developing listening skills that are attuned to the complexities of native speech. Through active listening exercises, transcription practice, varied accent exposure, and contextual listening, learners equip themselves with the tools necessary to navigate the auditory landscape of a new language with confidence and clarity. This approach fosters an enhanced capacity for comprehension, and a deeper appreciation for the intricate beauty of spoken language as learners come to recognize and revel in the nuances that define the sonic character of human expression.

Accent Reduction Techniques for Multilingual Learners

Accent, the unique melody of speech that roots us in culture and identity, is a formidable frontier for multilingual enthusiasts aiming for clarity and comprehensibility in new linguistic territories. The quest to smooth the edges of one's accent, not to erase but to refine, demands a nuanced, systematic approach. Far from mere mimicry, this endeavor is an intricate dance of auditory fine-tuning and muscular talent, a testament to the learner's dedication to authentic expression and intercultural dialogue.

Targeted Pronunciation Practice

In multilingual learning, pronunciation refinement is paved with the stones of targeted practice, a deliberate honing of those sounds and intonations that elude the learner's grasp. This process begins with an acute awareness of the phonetic landscape; a keen ear turned to the subtleties that distinguish native from non-native pronunciation. It's a meticulous segmentation of speech into its constituent sounds, each to be tackled precisely. For instance, the learner might isolate the trilled "r" sound prevalent in Spanish and Italian, dedicating time to its practice outside the flow of conversation to ensure accurate reproduction. This focused approach allows for the gradual assimilation of challenging phonemes into the learner's repertoire, ensuring that each sound is not just approximated but embodied with authenticity.

Recording and Self-Analysis

The journey toward accent reduction is deeply personal, demanding a mirror to reflect the nuances of one's spoken language. Here, the tool of choice is the recorder, an unassuming device that captures the contours of pronunciation, offering an objective perspective on the learner's speech. Regularly recording oneself, whether reciting prepared texts or engaging in spontaneous dialogue, provides a wealth of material for self-analysis. Listening back, the learner becomes both a critic and coach, identifying discrepancies between their speech and native speakers. This reflective practice, coupled with persistent effort, gradually bridges the gap, guiding the learner toward a pronunciation that resonates with the natural rhythm and melody of the target language.

Tongue Twisters and Speech Exercises

Tongue twisters and speech exercises stand out for their efficacy and inherent playfulness among the arsenal of techniques at the disposal of language learners. By their very design, these linguistic gymnastics challenge articulatory precision, speed, and agility, making them invaluable tools for accent reduction. Engaging with tongue twisters in the target language stretches the boundaries of comfort and familiarity, forcing the mouth and tongue into new configurations. Similarly, speech exercises emphasizing rhythm, stress, and intonation patterns offer a rhythmic understanding of speech that transcends mere vocabulary acquisition. Through repetition and practice, these exercises enhance articulatory accuracy and imbue the learner's speech with the natural cadence of the target language, a crucial step toward accent refinement.

Professional Guidance

While self-directed efforts form the backbone of accent reduction, the guidance of professionals in this field can accelerate progress, offering insights and corrections that might elude the solitary learner. Speech therapists and accent coaches, armed with a deep understanding of phonetics and articulatory mechanics, provide tailored strategies and feedback that address specific challenges faced by the learner. This expert intervention, often grounded in systematic assessment and targeted exercises, illuminates the path to pronunciation improvement, ensuring that efforts are efficient and effective. For learners committed to achieving significant gains in accent reduction, investing in professional guidance represents a strategic leveraging of resources, a decision that underscores the seriousness of their linguistic ambitions.

In navigating these waters, learners embrace a multifaceted strategy that marries self-directed practice with expert insight, underpinned by a commitment to authentic expression and intercultural respect. This journey, marked by targeted practice, reflective analysis, playful yet challenging exercises, and the pursuit of professional guidance, is a testament to the transformative power of diligent effort and strategic intervention in the quest for accent reduction. Through this process, learners refine their pronunciation and deepen their connection to the languages they seek to inhabit, fostering a mode of expression that bridges cultures and expands horizons.

The Power of Shadowing in Language Learning

In acquiring new languages, shadowing emerges as a method that intertwines the auditory with the verbal, a technique where learners echo the speech of native speakers in real-time, aiming to mirror not just words but the music behind them. This strategy, seemingly simple in its execution, unfolds layers of complexity and depth as one ventures deeper, revealing its potential to significantly elevate one's proficiency in a foreign language. Through shadowing, learners engage in a dynamic dialogue with the language that challenges and refines their auditory and vocal faculties in tandem.

At its core, shadowing involves the learner playing audio recordings of native speakers and attempting to replicate the speech simultaneously. This act of immediate repetition necessitates an acute focus and a high level of engagement, as the learner must process auditory information swiftly and produce the corresponding speech without pause. The choice of materials for this exercise is pivotal in its effectiveness. It requires a careful selection of content that aligns with the learner's current level of understanding yet pushes the boundaries of their comfort zone. For beginners, materials may consist of slow-paced dialogues or narratives with clear articulation, gradually advancing to faster, more complex speech as proficiency grows. This progression ensures that learners are continuously challenged, promoting growth in their listening and speaking abilities.

The cognitive and oral coordination demanded by shadowing is where its true challenge lies. Learners must split their attention between comprehension and articulation, a dual task that exercises the brain's capacity to process and produce language simultaneously. Regular practice in this manner enhances one's ability to decode spoken language quickly and respond with increasing speed and accuracy. This exercise in multitasking does not merely improve one's linguistic abilities but also sharpens cognitive functions more broadly, fostering skills that transcend language learning and infiltrate other areas of life.

Beyond the evident benefits to pronunciation, the shadowing

technique offers expansive rewards that extend into listening comprehension and speaking fluency. By engaging with the rhythm, intonation, and stress patterns of native speech, learners internalize the musicality of the language. This immersion in the auditory aspects of the language enriches the learner's understanding of its nuances, aiding in developing an ear for language sensitive to its subtleties. Such a refined auditory sense proves invaluable in real-life conversations, where the ability to discern slight variations in tone or stress can alter the meaning conveyed.

Moreover, shadowing propels learners into a realm of active language usage often missing from traditional study methods. By speaking alongside native speakers, learners break free from passive learning, stepping into an active role where language is absorbed and used. This transition from passive listener to active participant fosters speaking fluency as learners become more comfortable with the spontaneous production of language. Speaking, no matter how imperfectly, builds confidence and reduces the hesitancy that often accompanies the fear of making mistakes. In time, shadowing transforms the daunting task of speaking a new language into a natural, fluid extension of the learner's linguistic repertoire.

With its simplicity and depth, shadowing is a testament to the power of immersion and active practice in language learning. Through this technique, learners refine their pronunciation and listening skills and embark on a more dynamic and engaging path toward fluency. By demanding simultaneous comprehension and speech production, the shadowing method fosters linguistic agility and cognitive coordination that few other practices can match. It encourages learners to step beyond the role of passive recipients of knowledge, inviting them to become active co-creators in their language learning journey. In doing so, shadowing enhances linguistic proficiency. It cultivates a deeper, more intuitive connection with the language, where the learner moves in harmony with its rhythms and melodies, embodying the language as their own.

Utilizing Technology for Pronunciation Practice

In an age where the digital and linguistic worlds intertwine with increasing intimacy, the tools at our disposal for honing pronunciation in new languages evolve rapidly and are more sophisticated than previous generations might have imagined. This fusion of technological innovation with the age-old challenge of language acquisition opens up vistas of possibility for learners intent on refining their spoken word to mirror the fluidity and precision of native speakers.

Pronunciation Apps: A Gateway to Accurate Sounds

The proliferation of apps designed specifically for pronunciation practice represents a significant leap forward in language learning technology. These digital platforms serve not just as repositories of words and sounds but as interactive guides that lead learners through the intricacies of pronunciation with a precision that textbooks alone cannot offer.

Each app, with its library of phonetic exercises, presents a structured path toward vocal accuracy, using visual cues and instant feedback to correct mispronunciations. Through a process that often feels more like play than study, learners engage in repetitive drills that, over time, subtly adjust the tongue's posture and the mouth's shape to produce sounds once foreign, now familiar. The gamification of pronunciation practice within these apps adds an element of motivation, transforming the daunting task of mastering new sounds into a series of achievable, rewarding challenges.

Speech Recognition Software: The Mirror of Modernity

Speech recognition software stands at the cutting edge of pronunciation technology, offering learners an unflinching reflection of their spoken language capabilities. This software, embedded within language learning apps or standalone platforms, listens with an algorithmic ear to the nuances of the learner's speech, comparing it against the benchmark of native pronunciation. The immediate feedback such tools provide is granular and comprehensive, pinpointing the inaccuracies in sound production and often the rhythm and intonation patterns that distinguish native from non-native speech. This real-time critique, devoid of human subjectivity, allows learners to identify and focus on specific areas of weakness, turning the solitary practice act into an interactive dialogue with the digital tutor.

Online Tutors and Language Exchange: The Human Touch in the Digital Age

Despite the advances in artificial intelligence and algorithmic learning, the role of human interaction in language acquisition still needs to be improved. Online tutors and language exchange platforms bring the nuanced understanding and empathetic feedback of native speakers into the learner's home, bridging distances that once made such interaction a luxury. Video calls with tutors or exchange partners offer a safe, supportive environment where learners can test their pronunciation against the ears of those who know the language from the inside. These sessions, often structured to focus on specific pronunciation goals, provide corrections, encouragement, and strategies for overcoming chronic errors. The subtleties of humor, sarcasm, and cultural references, imbued in the intonation and stress patterns of speech, come to life in these exchanges, enriching the learner's understanding of the language as a living entity.

Audiovisual Materials: Engaging All Senses in the Quest for Pronunciation Mastery

Integrating audiovisual materials into pronunciation practice offers a multisensory learning experience that textbooks alone cannot replicate. Videos of native speakers, whether in formal language lessons or informal vlogs, present visual cues alongside auditory ones, illustrating the physical mechanics of sound production. Observing the movement of the lips, the placement of the tongue, and even the expressions accompanying certain sounds provides learners with a model to emulate, a visual blueprint to accompany the auditory guide. This combination of hearing and seeing creates a richer, more engaging learning experience, facilitating a deeper internalization of correct pronunciation. The accessibility of such materials, ranging from online courses to video-sharing platforms, ensures that learners can find resources tailored to their needs, making the pursuit of pronunciation excellence a journey informed and inspired by the wealth of human expression available at our fingertips.

In this digital era, the tools for mastering the pronunciation of new languages are as varied as they are effective, blending the analytical power of technology with the irreplaceable value of human interaction. Through apps, software, online tutoring, and audiovisual materials, learners can tackle pronunciation challenges with a comprehensive arsenal, turning the once formidable task into an achievable, even enjoyable pursuit. The path to pronunciation mastery, guided by these modern innovations, is marked by constant feedback, interactive learning, and the seamless integration of learning into daily life, ensuring that every effort brings the learner closer to the fluidity and authenticity of native speech.

Interactive Listening: Engaging with Content Actively

In language learning, listening transcends the mere auditory reception of words and phrases; it evolves into a vibrant, interactive dialogue with the content, demanding active participation that ignites the cognitive faculties in myriad ways. This engagement with listening materials is not a passive journey but a dynamic interaction, where the mind is constantly at play, deciphering, predicting, and synthesizing information gleaned from the auditory experience.

Engagement Strategies

The techniques for active engagement with listening materials are manifold, each designed to thrust the listener into the heart of the language learning process. Among these, summarizing content after listening sessions stands out for its ability to consolidate understanding and retention. This exercise compels the learner to distill the essence of what was heard into a coherent narrative, thereby reinforcing comprehension and memory. Predicting content, another potent strategy, primes the listener's anticipation of linguistic structures and vocabulary, fostering a readiness that enhances the listening experience. Engaging in these practices transforms listening from a solitary activity into an interactive exploration of language, where every sound heard is a piece in the giant puzzle of linguistic mastery.

Interactive Platforms

The digital age ushers in an array of interactive language learning platforms that weave listening comprehension into the fabric of their pedagogical approach. These platforms, rich audio materials, quizzes, and exercise repositories, are designed to immerse the learner in a simulated linguistic environment where listening is practiced and actively applied. Through activities that range from completing sentences based on audio cues to responding to questions in real-time, these platforms offer a scaffolded learning experience that gradually elevates the learner's auditory skills. Including immediate feedback mechanisms further refines the process, allowing learners to identify areas of weakness and adjust their strategies accordingly.

Language Learning Games

The introduction of games into the language learning equation infuses the process with fun and competition that significantly boosts engagement and motivation. These games, often available on various digital platforms, are crafted to enhance listening skills entertainingly and educationally. From matching spoken words with their written counterparts to navigating through story-based challenges guided by audio instructions, these games offer a playful yet practical approach to improving listening comprehension. The interactive nature of these games,

137

coupled with the immediate rewards for success, creates a learning environment that is stimulating and rewarding, encouraging the learner to delve deeper into the auditory aspects of the language.

Discussion and Analysis

The culmination of the interactive listening process frequently manifests in the discussion and analysis of the content with peers or tutors. This dialogue, whether in person or through digital communication channels, allows learners to articulate their understanding, pose questions, and exchange interpretations. Such discussions reinforce comprehension and enhance critical thinking and analytical skills as learners dissect the linguistic and thematic elements of the content. The collaborative nature of these discussions fosters a sense of community among learners, offering support and encouragement as they navigate the complexities of the language. Moreover, the insights gained from tutors and more proficient speakers offer invaluable perspectives that enrich the learner's understanding and appreciation of the language.

In navigating the landscape of interactive listening, learners embark on a journey rich with opportunities for engagement, discovery, and growth. Listening is transformed through strategies that demand active participation, platforms that simulate immersive linguistic environments, games that marry fun with learning, and discussions that deepen understanding. It becomes an adventure that challenges the mind, sharpens the ear, and ultimately unlocks the full potential of the learner's linguistic capabilities.

The Role of Music and Lyrics in Language Learning

In the tapestry of language acquisition, melodies and lyrics stand as vibrant threads, weaving through the fabric of linguistic development with elegance and efficacy. This harmonic approach to learning encompasses not just the acquisition of new vocabulary but also the rhythmic mastery of pronunciation, the nuanced comprehension of cultural context, and the reinforcement of memory through the universal language of music.

Lyrical Analysis

Dissecting song lyrics offers a gateway into the heart of a language, revealing layers of meaning, expressions, and grammatical intricacies often missed in conventional study. This analytical exercise invites learners to parse through verses, choruses, and bridges, unearthing hidden linguistic gems. Each line of a song becomes a lesson in syntax and semantics as learners scrutinize the choice of words, their arrangement, and their contribution to the piece's overall message. This meticulous examination of lyrics demystifies idiomatic expressions and colloquialisms, granting learners insights into the informal registers of the language seldom explored in textbooks. The process extends beyond mere analysis; it invites learners to engage with the language creatively, encouraging them to pen their interpretations or compose responses, thereby deepening their connection with the linguistic and cultural essence of the song.

Sing-Along for Pronunciation

Singing along to music in the target language transcends simple vocalization; it is an exercise in phonetic precision and rhythmic fluency. Music, with its inherent cadence and melody, aids learners in navigating the prosodic features of the language, from intonation patterns to stress placement. This melodic mimicry facilitates a more natural pronunciation, as learners instinctively match their vocal output to the musical model. The repetition inherent in singing, particularly with catchy, repetitive choruses, ensures that learners practice complex sounds and phrases within the supportive scaffold of rhythm and melody. This enjoyable and immersive practice subtly refines the learner's accent, edging them closer to the elusive goal of native-like pronunciation without the drudgery often associated with phonetic drills.

Cultural Insights through Music

Music reflects the culture from which it springs, offering listeners a window into people's values, emotions, and historical narratives. For language learners, engaging with music as a cultural artifact provides a rich context for understanding the language's usage and nuances. Songs often capture the essence of an era, the collective hopes and fears of a society, or the timeless themes that resonate across generations. By exploring the thematic content of music, learners gain access to the cultural underpinnings of the language, insights that textbooks can only hint at. This exploration might lead learners down paths less traveled to genres and artists that embody the diversity of the language's cultural landscape. In doing so, learners not only expand their linguistic repertoire but also foster a deeper appreciation for the culture that shapes and is shaped by the language.

Memory Aid

The mnemonic power of music is well-documented, with melodies and rhythms proven to enhance recall and retention. For language learners, this attribute of music serves as a potent tool for embedding vocabulary, phrases, and grammatical structures into memory. With their repetitive structures and memorable hooks, catchy tunes create a mental scaffold upon which linguistic information can be effortlessly hung. This process transforms the act of memorization from a tedious chore into an enjoyable activity, as learners find themselves recalling language through the medium of song. Furthermore, the emotional resonance of music amplifies its mnemonic effectiveness; songs that evoke feelings or are associated with specific experiences etch the accompanying language more deeply into the learner's memory.

Thus, music becomes not just a source of linguistic input but a vessel for ensuring that the language learned is not easily forgotten, embedding itself in the learner's consciousness through the dual channels of melody and emotion.

Music emerges as a multifaceted ally in this harmonious approach to language learning, enriching the learner's journey with its lyrical depth, phonetic rhythm, cultural resonance, and mnemonic strength. Through lyrical analysis, sing-along exercises, artistic exploration, and the leveraging of music as a memory aid, learners unlock a symphonic method of language acquisition. This immersive and enjoyable method elevates learning from a mechanical accumulation of knowledge to an artistic exploration of sound, meaning, and culture. In language learning, music stands not on the periphery but at the core, a melodic bridge to linguistic fluency and cultural understanding.

Overcoming the Plateau in Listening Comprehension

A plateau in listening comprehension can often feel like a vast, insurmountable wall, halting progress with its daunting presence. Yet, what initially appears as an obstacle is merely a signpost, signaling the need for a shift in strategies, a diversification of materials, and a reaffirmation of commitment to the nuanced craft of understanding spoken language at deeper levels.

Implementing more advanced listening strategies becomes

necessary as proficiency grows. This evolution in approach involves an intentional shift towards engaging with content that stretches the listener's capabilities, pushing them into the zone of proximal development where genuine growth occurs. It's similar to a musician practicing slightly above their skill level; the challenge invigorates the mind, sparking adaptations that lead to an expanded range of comprehension. This might involve dissecting complex dialogues for underlying meanings, identifying rhetorical devices in speeches, or interpreting the emotional undertones in narratives. Each task requires a listener to employ critical thinking and inferential reasoning with linguistic understanding, enriching their auditory skills with layers of analytical depth.

Expanding the range of listening materials is pivotal in breaking through the plateau. The vast landscape of auditory content available, from podcasts discussing abstract concepts and lectures on diverse subjects to debates that showcase the ebb and flow of arguments, offers a treasure trove of opportunities for listening practice. Diversifying the types of listening materials prevents the stagnation of skills and introduces the learner to various linguistic registers, speaking speeds, and accents. This broad exposure ensures that the learner's listening abilities are not narrowly confined to specific contexts but are adaptable and robust, capable of navigating the complexities of language in its many forms.

Setting specific listening goals for each session is crucial for systematic progress. Rather than approaching listening practice with a vague aim of "improvement," defining clear, achievable objectives for each listening activity sharpens the focus and enhances the effectiveness of the training. Whether it's understanding the main argument of a lecture, noting the use of idiomatic expressions in a conversation, or identifying the tone and mood of a narrative, each goal acts as a beacon, guiding the listener's attention to specific aspects of the language. This targeted approach ensures that listening sessions are productive, with each session contributing to a gradual but definite advancement in comprehension skills.

Patience and persistence form the bedrock upon which breakthroughs in listening comprehension are built. Recognizing that significant improvements often unfold over extended periods of dedicated practice is essential for maintaining motivation and commitment. The journey is less about swift leaps in ability and more about the accumulation of incremental gains that, over time, coalesce into profound mastery. It is a process that demands resilience, acknowledging that progress is not always linear and that setbacks are mere stepping stones to greater understanding.

In this pursuit of elevated listening comprehension, the listener weaves together advanced strategies, a rich tapestry of materials, focused goals, and an unwavering dedication to the craft. The journey transcends mere practice, evolving into a deep exploration of language in its auditory form, immersing in the subtleties and complexities that define human communication. Through this dedicated endeavor, the plateau that once seemed an insurmountable barrier becomes a milestone, marking the transition to higher realms of linguistic insight and understanding.

As we conclude this exploration of strategies to enhance listening comprehension, it is evident that the process is complex yet deeply rewarding. Each step is integral to overcoming plateaus, from the infusion of advanced techniques to the deliberate selection of diverse materials, the setting of precise goals, and the cultivation of patience. This journey, rich in challenges and discoveries, mirrors the broader adventure of language learning, a continuous negotiation between effort and insight, between the known and the yet-to-be-discovered. As we move forward, let us carry the lessons learned, the strategies honed, and the resilience forged into the next chapter of our linguistic odyssey, ever open to the possibilities on the horizon.

7

Chapter 6: Sculpting Memory Palaces

In the labyrinth of the mind, where thoughts wander, and memories hide in shadowed corners, there exists a method as ancient as the hills, yet as fresh as the morning dew, for anchoring language in the bedrock of our consciousness. This method, known as the Method of Loci, transforms the abstract into the tangible and the forgotten into the unforgettable. With roots stretching back to the orators of ancient Greece, this technique offers a bridge across time, inviting modern language learners to traverse its span.

The Method of Loci: A Memory Palace for Languages

Imagine strolling through your childhood home, each room vivid with detail, each object a beacon of memories. Now, envision transforming this space into a repository for language, where every nook cradles a new word, and every corridor unfolds into sentences. This is the essence of the

Method of Loci, a spatial memory technique that leverages familiar environments to anchor and recall language information.

Spatial Memory Technique

The human brain's capacity to recall spatial environments exceeds its ability to remember isolated facts or disconnected data. By utilizing familiar spatial environments, such as a childhood home or a well-trodden path through a local park, learners can create mental frameworks for organizing and retrieving language elements. Each room or landmark within this mental landscape can serve as a container for different aspects of language, from vocabulary to grammatical rules.

Visualization and Association

Creating vivid associations between language elements and specific locations within the memory palace is crucial. For instance, associating the word "water" with the image of a fountain in a garden or linking the concept of past tense verbs with the stairs leading down to a basement embeds linguistic information within a sensory-rich context. These associations, strengthened by the brain's propensity for visual memory, ensure that language elements are memorized and experienced.

Application for Vocabulary and Grammar

The memory palace's scalability allows for incorporating both vocabulary and grammatical structures. A learner might designate one room for nouns related to food, another for verbs of movement, while a hallway might be lined with the conjugations of an irregular verb. As proficiency grows and the need for more complex language elements arises, additional rooms or new buildings can be constructed within the mental landscape, each tailored to house specific linguistic content.

Scalability

As language proficiency expands, so too does the complexity of the information needing storage. The beauty of the memory palace lies in its infinite scalability. Initially, a single room might suffice for basic vocabulary; however, as one delves deeper into the language, entire wings or new floors can be added to accommodate advanced vocabulary, idiomatic expressions, and complex grammatical structures. This adaptability ensures that the memory palace grows with the learner's linguistic journey, offering a flexible and enduring framework for language mastery.

Visual Element: Interactive Memory Palace Builder

To bring the method to life, an interactive memory palace builder offers learners a tangible tool for constructing their personal language landscapes. This digital platform allows users to select from various pre-designed spaces or upload images of their environments, then drag and drop language elements—represented by icons or flashcards—into specific locations. This tool not only aids in the initial creation of the memory palace but also provides a means for revisiting and expanding one's linguistic domain, reinforcing the connection between space, imagery, and language.

In harnessing the power of the Method of Loci, we find not just a technique for memory enhancement but a pathway to more profound linguistic intuition. By grounding language in the concrete and familiar, this method bridges the gap between knowing words and living them, transforming the act of recall into a journey through a landscape rich with personal meaning and linguistic discovery. Through constructing memory palaces, learners unlock the potential to elevate their language skills from mere recollection to vibrant, living knowledge.

Advanced Flashcard Strategies: Beyond Basic Vocabulary

In language acquisition, the humble flashcard, often under-estimated, wields an extraordinary capacity to anchor words and phrases within the folds of memory. Yet, to unlock the full potential of this tool, one must venture beyond merely scribbling words on cardstock. The evolution of flashcard techniques, propelled by the digital age, invites learners into a sophisticated dance of cognitive reinforcement, where algorithms, multimedia enhancements, and strategic organization converge to sculpt a robust linguistic foundation.

Spaced Repetition Software (SRS): Maximizing Retention with Flashcards Through Spaced Repetition Algorithms

At the heart of this modernized approach lies Spaced Repetition Software (SRS), a beacon guiding learners through the thickets of forgetfulness. By employing algorithms that adapt to an individual's learning pace, SRS platforms ensure that each linguistic element resurfaces at intervals optimized for memory consolidation. This digital orchestration of timing, which might present a word just as it teeters on the brink of being forgotten, reinforces retention in a manner that static flashcards cannot. The elegance of SRS lies in its ability to tailor review schedules to the learner's responses, creating a personalized path through the language landscape that is both efficient and profoundly effective.

Multimedia Flashcards: Incorporating Images, Audio, and Example Sentences into Flashcards for Richer Context

Infusing multimedia elements into flashcards transforms these learning aids from mere textual vessels into rich sensory experiences. By embedding images, the learner's visual cortex is enlisted in the task of language retention, allowing for deeper imprinting of words and phrases. Similarly, incorporating audio clips of native speakers pronouncing the words or phrases in question enriches the auditory dimension of learning, mirroring the natural language acquisition process. Furthermore, including example sentences offer context, illustrating the word's use within the tapestry of conversation or narrative. This multimedia approach enhances memory and fosters a more nuanced understanding of language as learners engage with words through multiple sensory channels.

Interleaved Practice Flashcards: Mixing Flashcards from Different Languages or Language Aspects to Enhance Cognitive Flexibility

For those navigating the waters of multilingualism, interleaved practice flashcards offer a robust strategy for enhancing cognitive flexibility. By shuffling flashcards from various languages or intertwining cards that cover different linguistic aspects— such as vocabulary, grammar, and idioms —learners encourage their brains to remain agile, constantly adjusting to shifts in linguistic context. This method mirrors the dynamic nature of real-world language use, where the ability to switch between languages or navigate varied linguistic situations is invaluable. Interleaved practice strengthens memory and prepares the learner for the fluidity required in multilingual communication, making it a potent tool in the polyglot's arsenal.

Personalization: Creating Personalized Flashcards That Cater to Individual Learning Needs and Preferences

At its core, the power of the flashcard lies in its potential for personalization. Tailoring flashcards to one's unique learning journey—whether by selecting words that resonate personally, crafting example sentences that reflect one's experiences, or choosing images that spark joy—makes language learning profoundly personal and engaging. This customization extends to the method of organization, allowing learners to group flashcards in a way that aligns with their learning objectives, be it thematic clusters, grammatical categories, or difficulty levels. By actively creating and curating their flashcards, learners forge a deeper connection with the language, transforming passive absorption into an act of creative expression.

In this landscape of advanced flashcard strategies, learners find themselves equipped with sophisticated tools that are intimately tailored to their journey. The dance of cognitive reinforcement becomes a celebration of personal growth and linguistic exploration, with each flashcard not just a step toward mastery but a reflection of the learner's unique path through the world of language.

Memory Techniques for Grammar: Making Rules Stick

Grammar is the scaffold in the arena where language architecture is constructed and deconstructed. Often perceived as a labyrinth of rules and exceptions, this intricate framework can elevate understanding or ensnare the unwary learner in its complexity. To navigate this terrain with agility, one must employ strategies that transform grammatical learning from a rote exercise into an intuitive grasp of linguistic patterns.

Grammar Mnemonics: Designing Mnemonics for Complex Grammatical Rules to Simplify Learning and Recall

The crafting of mnemonics, a technique as old as memory itself, serves as a beacon in the fog for those endeavoring to internalize the convolutions of grammar. The learner weaves a tapestry of cognitive shortcuts that facilitate rapid recall by distilling complex grammatical rules into simple, memorable phrases or acronyms. Consider, for instance, the challenge of remembering the sequence of tenses in English conditional sentences. A mnemonic such as "If I were rich, I would travel the world" encapsulates the structure in a nugget of imagery and desire, making the abstract rule concrete and personal. This mnemonic creation process serves as a mnemonic device and a creative act, embedding the rule within the learner's cognitive landscape through the dual threads of logic and emotion.

Pattern Recognition: Leveraging the Brain's Natural Inclination for Pattern Recognition to Understand Grammatical Structures

With its preference for discerning patterns amidst the chaos, human cognition finds fertile ground in studying grammar. By illuminating the patterns that underlie grammatical structures, learners can anticipate rather than memorize rules, seeing grammar not as a collection of arbitrary mandates but as a coherent system governed by logic. This approach requires a shift in perspective from viewing grammar as a barrier to understanding it as a puzzle where each piece fits within a predictable framework. Training the mind to recognize these patterns involves active engagement with the language in its natural state—through reading, listening, and conversation— allowing the learner to infer rules from context and repetition. In this way, pattern recognition transforms grammar learning from a task of memorization to one of discovery, where each grammatical structure reveals itself as part of a larger, intelligible whole.

Active Usage: Creating Opportunities for Active Use of New Grammar Rules to Solidify Understanding and Memory

The leap from theoretical knowledge to practical application marks the transition from learning to mastery of grammar. Active usage of newly acquired grammatical structures cements understanding, allowing the learner to test the boundaries and flexibilities of the rules within the playful arena of language use. This might manifest in the composition of sentences that incorporate the target structure, the deliberate alteration of sentences to reflect different grammatical moods or aspects, or the engagement in language exchange where these structures can be employed in real-time dialogue. Through this process, grammar transcends the page, becoming a tool wielded with intention and creativity. Using grammar in context reinforces memory and deepens the learner's intuitive sense of how the language operates, blending the art of communication with the science of structure.

Contextual Learning: Embedding Grammatical Structures in Meaningful Contexts Rather Than Memorizing in Isolation

The final strand in this tapestry of the grammatical acquisition lies in embedding structures within meaningful contexts. Stripping the grammar of its abstraction and placing it within the narrative flow of real-life situations, stories, or personal anecdotes imbues it with relevance. This method leverages the brain's propensity for story-driven learning, where information framed within the context of a narrative or personal connection is more readily absorbed and retained. By associating a grammatical structure with a specific context—be it a memorable event, a piece of literature, or a cultural artifact— the learner anchors the rule within a web of associations, making recall not an act of rote retrieval but a journey through a landscape rich with meaning. This contextual embedding of grammar transforms it from a dry set of rules to a vibrant thread in the communication fabric, woven seamlessly into the learner's expanding linguistic repertoire.

In this multifaceted approach to grammar, where mnemonics provide the scaffolding, pattern recognition, blueprint, active usage of the materials, and contextual learning of the site, learners construct their understanding of grammatical structures with precision and creativity. Through these techniques, grammar sheds its guise as a formidable adversary, revealing itself instead as a map to be navigated, a puzzle to be solved, and, ultimately, a structure to be inhabited with confidence and fluency.

Harnessing the Power of Visual Memory in Language Learning

In the vast expanse of cognitive science, visual memory stands as a towering beacon, illuminating paths through the dense forests of language acquisition. This domain, rich with color and form, offers fertile ground for sowing the seeds of linguistic knowledge, where imagery and text intertwine to create a lush learning landscape. Within this realm, associating words with solid visual images emerges as a method and a transformative practice, elevating the mundane into the realm of the unforgettable.

Imagery for Vocabulary

Binding vocabulary to imagery is akin to painting with words; each brush stroke brings a concept to life, marrying the abstract with the tangible. This fusion of language and image transcends simple memorization, embedding words deep within the visual cortex. Once abstract and elusive, a word becomes as vivid and immediate as a cherished photograph. For instance, the word "liberté" could be anchored in the mind's eye with the image of a fluttering French flag against a clear blue sky, each ripple of the fabric echoing the concept of freedom. Such associations do not merely linger on the surface of memory but seep into its very fibers, ensuring that words are not just remembered but felt, their meanings resonant with imagery.

158

Mind Maps for Language Concepts

Creating mind maps for organizing language rules, vocabulary themes, and connections employs our cognition's spatial and visual strengths, transforming the linear into the dynamic. Each mind map becomes a living entity, branches spreading out to link concepts and ideas flowering from the nodes of thought. This visually striking and intellectually engaging method allows for exploring language in a structured and freeform manner. A mind map could, for instance, chart the journey of conjugations and tenses around the hub of a verb, each pathway leading to different uses and contexts, creating a visual narrative of the word's life within the language. Through this process, the complexity of language is rendered not as a barrier but as a landscape to be navigated, with each map offering a bird's-eye view of linguistic terrain.

Color Coding

The application of color coding in distinguishing between languages, grammatical genders, or linguistic features taps into the brain's inherent sensitivity to color as a means of categorization and recall. In this chromatic schema, each hue becomes a key, unlocking domains of language with a glance. Blue might become the emblem of masculine nouns, pink of feminine, turning a table of words into a visual mosaic that speaks of gender with color. When applied across multiple languages, this system paints a rainbow of grammar and vocabulary, with each language a different spectrum and each grammatical aspect a shade within. This method not only aids in differentiation but also recall, with the brain associating linguistic elements with their respective colors, a tapestry of language woven into the loom of memory.

Visual Storytelling

The crafting of visual narratives that incorporate new language elements elevates the act of learning into the realm of creation. Each narrative, a tapestry of images and words, tells a story that is both a journey through language and a voyage of the imagination. A learner may create a comic strip where each frame serves as a stage for new vocabulary and grammar, the narrative thread binding the linguistic elements into a coherent whole. This immersive and creative process allows for exploring language within the story's context, where each new word or grammatical structure is learned and lived. Through the lens of visual storytelling, language becomes not a subject to be studied. Still, a world to be inhabited, each narrative a path through the forests of language, lit by the lantern of imagery.

In this exploration of visual memory in language learning, where imagery, mind maps, color coding, and visual narratives converge, we find not just strategies for learning but portals to deeper understanding. These methods, rich with color and form, transform the landscape of language acquisition, inviting learners to step beyond the confines of conventional study into a realm where language is not just seen but experienced. In this realm, each word, each grammatical rule, and each linguistic nuance becomes a brushstroke in the ever-expanding canvas of knowledge, a masterpiece in the making, guided by the hand of visual memory.

The Link Method: Connecting New Words to Known Concepts

In the complicated expanse of the mind, where the tendrils of memory weave through the substratum of consciousness, there exists an ancient and intuitive method for anchoring the rubble of new language amidst the jetsam of the known. This technique, known as the Link Method, operates on the premise that the mind, a tapestry of interconnected threads, finds solace and strength in creating associations. By forging chains between newly encountered language elements and the familiar bedrock of existing knowledge, this method does not simply suggest a path through the thicket of language acquisition; it lights a torch, illuminating the shadows cast by the unfamiliar.

Association Chains

To envisage the construction of association chains, one might consider the mind an architect, linking new words to concepts or images already residing within the mental repository.

This process, intricate in its simplicity, demands a deliberate engagement with each new linguistic fragment, binding it to a known counterpart by creating a vivid, often visceral, mental image. For instance, the Spanish word "gato" (cat) might be linked to the image of one's childhood pet, a particular alley cat, or even a beloved character from a novel, thus anchoring the foreign term in the fertile ground of personal experience. The strength of these chains lies not in their logical coherence but in their emotional resonance, the vividness of the imagery acting as a catalyst for recall.

Creative and Absurd Associations

The terrain of memory is one where the bizarre and the outlandish often hold sway, their flagrant disregard for the mundane rendering them luminous in the twilight of forgetfulness. In this context, the Link Method thrives on creating associations that are not merely unusual but border on the absurd. The more unpredictable the connection, the more memorable its imprint upon the memory. A word such as "Volare" (to fly in Italian) might find its anchor in the ludicrous image of a penguin piloting an airplane, the absurdity of the scene ensuring its permanence in memory. This embrace of the creative and the nonsensical serves as a testament to the mind's capacity for innovation and its ability to find footholds for the new within the crevices of the known. However improbable those connections may seem.

Application Across Languages

For the polyglot, the Link Method offers a bridge that spans the divide between languages, creating a network of pathways that meander through the multilingual landscape. By establishing links between similar words in different target languages, this method aids in retention and the discernment of linguistic patterns, the echoes of similarity serving as guideposts. For instance, the German word "Wasser" and the Spanish "agua" might be linked to the image of a specific river, its flow connecting the disparate linguistic elements in the stream of consciousness. This cross-linguistic application of the Link Method streamlines the language acquisition process and weaves a tapestry of connections that enriches the learner's linguistic repertoire, each linking a thread in the broader mosaic of multilingualism.

Reinforcement through Repetition

The tapestry, once woven, demands not merely admiration but care, the threads of association requiring reinforcement lest they fray in the tumult of daily cognition. In this light, the Link Method finds its complement in the diligent practice of repetition, the periodic revisitation of associations to tighten the weave. This reinforcement, however, is not a mere rote rehearsal but an active engagement with the imagery and connections previously established, a rekindling of the initial spark of association. Through this practice, once tentative, the chains of connection become ironclad, the links so entrenched in the fabric of memory that they resist the erosive forces of time and distraction. In this repetition, this deliberate circling back to the anchors we have cast, the true power of the Link Method is realized, transforming fleeting encounters with language into enduring tenets of our linguistic landscape.

In the realm where words flutter like moths around the flame of understanding, the Link Method stands as a beacon, guiding the way through the darkness. By forging connections between the new and the known, embracing the creative and the absurd, applying these principles across the spectrum of languages, and reinforcing the woven fabric of memory through repetition, this method transcends the boundaries of traditional language learning. It is an invitation to dance in the spaces between the known and the unknown, to find harmony in the dissonance of unfamiliarity, and to anchor the fleeting whispers of new languages in the enduring chorus of memory.

Chunking for Languages: Mastering Phrases, Not Just Words

In the intricate dance of language acquisition, where each word is a step and every grammatical rule a turn, a technique moves beyond memorizing an isolated lexicon into holistic understanding. This technique, known as chunking, invites learners to embrace phrases and sentences in their entirety, absorbing them as complete units of meaning rather than disjointed fragments of speech. Through this approach, the mind, ever so adept at seeking patterns and making connections, finds a more natural and fluid pathway to linguistic proficiency.

Phrase-Based Learning

At the heart of phrase-based learning is the recognition of language as a living entity that thrives not in the isolation of words but in the community of phrases. Engaging with language at the level of phrases means tapping into the rhythmic flow of communication, where meaning is conveyed not by single words but by their constellations, each phrase a galaxy of intention and nuance. This method acknowledges that in the wild terrains of everyday conversation, language reveals itself in clusters of words that provide vocabulary and a blueprint for expression when learned as whole chunks. It's akin to learning the chords of a song rather than individual notes, where the harmony of the entire elevates the significance of each component.

Cognitive Load Reduction

The brilliance of chunking lies in its ability to lighten the cognitive load that often burdens learners, especially those navigating the multifaceted landscape of multilingualism. Internalizing language in chunks relieves the brain of the laborious task of assembling speech word by word, which can stifle fluency and spontaneity. Instead, phrases serve as ready-made building blocks of communication, instantly accessible and easily adaptable to various contexts. This reduced mental strain opens up cognitive bandwidth for higher-order tasks such as listening comprehension and contextual interpretation, allowing learners to engage with language more dynamically and responsively.

Natural Language Patterns

Delving into chunking is to engage in a subtle yet profound exploration of natural language patterns and collocations, those habitual pairings of words that native speakers wield with intuitive grace. Learning language in chunks is to attune oneself to these patterns, recognizing how words naturally coalesce into phrases and sentences. This method mirrors the organic process through which children acquire their first language, absorbing phrases whole and employing them in appropriate contexts without conscious analysis of their constituent parts. By aligning language learning with this innate propensity for pattern recognition, chunking not only accelerates the acquisition of linguistic fluency but also deepens the learner's intuitive grasp of the language's rhythm and logic.

Application in Speaking and Writing

The true potency of chunking unfolds in the active application of learned phrases in both speaking and writing, where the pre-fabricated blocks of language are assembled into structures of communication that reflect the learner's intent and personality. In speaking, these chunks become the scaffolding for spontaneous dialogue, allowing learners to navigate conversations fluently and confidently that word-by-word construction could never afford. In writing, chunking serves as a framework for composition, where phrases are woven together to create coherent, engaging, and stylistically appropriate texts. This practice reinforces the learner's familiarity with the chunks and encourages experimentation and adaptation as learners remix, modify, and expand upon the phrases to suit their expressive needs.

In the embrace of chunking, learners discover a pathway to language mastery that is both efficient and enriching, a method that acknowledges the complexity of language while offering a strategy for navigating it with elegance and ease. Through the integration of phrase-based learning, the strategic reduction of cognitive load, the exploration of natural language patterns, and the active application of chunks in speaking and writing, this approach offers a blueprint for linguistic proficiency that is holistic, dynamic, and deeply rooted in the authentic use of language. In this way, chunking facilitates the acquisition of new languages and enriches the learner's engagement with the world through nuanced, fluent communication.

167

Repetition Patterns for Long-term Retention

In the nuanced tapestry of language learning, repetition serves as the weft thread, intertwining with the warp of comprehension to create a resilient and prosperous fabric of knowledge. Within this framework, the meticulous crafting of repetition schedules emerges as a vital tool, akin to a gardener's calendar, guiding the cyclic nurturing of linguistic seeds to ensure their bloom into complete fluency.

Designing Repetition Schedules

The architecture of effective repetition schedules draws inspiration from the natural rhythms of memory decay, aligning the reintroduction of language elements with the junctures at which they begin to fade from the mind's grasp. This alignment, rooted in the psychological principle of spaced repetition, transforms the act of review from a mundane task into a strategic reinforcement of neural pathways. Imagine, for instance, the precision with which a conductor leads an orchestra; each cue timed to elicit the perfect harmony; similarly, a well-structured repetition schedule orchestrates the learner's engagement with language, each review session timed to optimize retention and recall.

Incremental Difficulty

In language learning, the gradual escalation of challenge is crucial in maintaining engagement and facilitating growth. When applied to repetition patterns, this principle of incremental difficulty ensures that learners are energized by simplicity and manageable complexity. It is the linguistic equivalent of scaling a mountain, where each camp is set higher than the last, pushing the boundaries of one's linguistic altitude without risking the peril of discouragement. Through the careful calibration of language elements introduced for review, from the foundational to the sophisticated, learners experience a steady ascent in proficiency, each repetition session a step up the linguistic incline.

Active Recall Techniques

The dynamism of active recall techniques injects vitality into the process of repetition, transforming it from passive review to active engagement. This approach demands that learners retrieve language elements from the depths of memory without the crutch of visual or textual cues. This task strengthens mental connections and enhances recall efficiency. Consider the challenge posed by a blank canvas to an artist; similarly, active recall confronts the learner with the task of painting the details of language from memory, each effort to retrieve and articulate a word or phrase serving to deepen its imprint in the cognitive landscape. Through

169

self-generated testing or the oral recitation of language elements in varied contexts, active recall ensures that repetition is not a mere echo of past learning but a re-creation, each iteration a reinforcement of memory's architecture.

Cross-Language Review Sessions

For those who navigate the waters of multilingualism, the balanced repetition of multiple languages poses a unique challenge, akin to an acrobat maintaining equilibrium across parallel tightropes. Cross-language review sessions, designed to distribute attention evenly across languages, prevent the dominance of one language at the expense of others, ensuring that proficiency is maintained and advanced across the linguistic spectrum. In these sessions, the learner engages in a deliberate rotation through languages, each review cycle a weave through the tapestry of their multilingual landscape. This method mirrors the fluidity required in real-world multilingual settings, where the ability to switch between languages easily is paramount. Through the strategic alternation of focus, learners cultivate a balanced linguistic garden, where no language withers from neglect nor overshadows the rest in its growth.

In the cultivation of long-term retention, these methodologies — each a thread in the larger weave of language learning— combine to create a repetition pattern that is both structured and dynamic. The schedule, rooted in the science of memory decay, provides the framework; the incremental increase in difficulty ensures that the learning landscape is ever-expanding; active recall techniques infuse the process with energy and efficacy; and cross-language review sessions maintain the equilibrium of multilingual proficiency. Together, they form a holistic approach to repetition that transcends mere review, elevating it to an art form that nurtures the roots of language deep in the fertile ground of memory, ensuring that the fruits of linguistic knowledge are abundant and enduring.

Memory Games for Multilingual Learners

In the multifaceted realm of multilingual education, incorporating games tailored specifically for enhancing memory represents a novel convergence of entertainment and pedagogy. These games, meticulously designed to bolster the retention of linguistic elements, offer a dynamic alternative to traditional memorization methods, infusing the process with joy and interactive engagement. Through the strategic application of these games, learners discover not just a method of study but a playground for the mind, where language acquisition unfolds with the spontaneity and thrill of play.

Language Learning Games: Introducing Games Specifically Designed to Improve Memory for Language Learners

The genesis of language learning games marks a pivotal moment in educational methodologies, shifting the paradigm from rote learning to an experiential process of discovery and reinforcement. These games, ranging from digital applications to board games, are crafted with the dual purpose of captivating the learner's attention and embedding linguistic information within the cognitive matrix. Engaging with these games, learners encounter various linguistic challenges, each designed to test memory in a context that mimics real-life language use. This immersive approach ensures that every interaction, every decision, and every victory reinforces the neural pathways as- sociated with the target language, embedding words, phrases, and grammatical structures within the fabric of long-term memory.

Customizable Memory Challenges: Creating Customizable Memory Challenges That Can Be Adjusted for Different Languages and Proficiency Levels

The flexibility inherent in customizable memory challenges allows for a personalized approach to language learning, where the difficulty and content can be tailored to the individual's current level of proficiency and linguistic goals. This adaptability ensures that learners of all stages, from novices to advanced speakers, find relevance and challenge in the games they engage with. Customizable challenges involve manipulating game parameters to include specific vocabulary sets, grammatical structures, or thematic content, allowing learners to focus on areas of particular interest or difficulty. This personalization not only enhances the effectiveness of the learning experience but also fosters a sense of ownership over the process, motivating learners to push the boundaries of their linguistic capabilities.

Social Memory Exercises: Engaging in Social Memory
Exercises with Fellow Language Learners for Mutual
Reinforcement

The communal aspect of social memory exercises introduces
a collaborative dimension to language learning, where
learners come together physically or virtually to participate in
memory-enhancing activities. These exercises, which range
from competitive quizzes to cooperative storytelling games,
leverage the power of social interaction to reinforce linguistic
knowledge. In the shared space of these exercises, learners
find not just opponents and allies but mirrors reflecting their
linguistic journeys, offering insights, corrections, and
encouragement. This social reinforcement, mediated through
the medium of play, strengthens not only individual memory
but also the collective linguistic knowledge of the group,
creating a community of learners bound together by the
shared pursuit of multilingual proficiency.

Digital and Physical Games: Utilizing Both Digital Apps and Physical Games to Cater to Different Learning Environments and Preferences

In modern language education, the distinction between digital and physical realms offers learners a spectrum of modalities for engaging with memory games. Digital applications provide the convenience of accessibility, allowing learners to engage with language learning games anytime, anywhere, with the added benefits of interactive feedback and the ability to connect with a global community of learners. Conversely, physical games offer a tactile experience, where handling cards, moving pieces, and interacting face-to-face with fellow players adds a dimension of sensory engagement to the learning process. This dichotomy between digital and physical allows learners to choose the modality that best suits their environment, preferences, and learning style, ensuring that the pursuit of linguistic proficiency is versatile and inclusive.

In navigating the diverse landscape of memory games for multilingual learners, individuals encounter a rich tapestry of opportunities for linguistic reinforcement, each game a thread woven into the broader fabric of language acquisition. Through the strategic application of language-specific games, the customization of challenges to align with personal goals, the collaborative energy of social memory exercises, and the integration of both digital and physical modalities, learners unlock a realm where education transcends the confines of traditional methodologies, morphing into an experience that is as enriching as it is enjoyable.

This fusion of play and instruction enhances the retention of linguistic knowledge and rekindles the intrinsic joy of learning, reminding us that at the heart of language lies not just a tool for communication but a bridge to understanding, a source of connection, and a path to discovery.

As we close this chapter, we reflect on the journey through the innovative landscape of memory strategies, acknowledging the transformative power of games in language learning. Exploring these dynamic methodologies underscores the profound potential for growth, engagement, and mastery inherent in the playful pursuit of multilingualism. In the following chapters, we continue to unravel the intricacies of language acquisition, guided by the knowledge that the quest for fluency is not just a challenge to be met but an adventure to be embraced.

Chapter 7: Weaving Languages into the Fabric of Daily Life

In language learning, the monumental often resides in the minute—the grand pursuit of fluency finds its foundation in accumulating everyday habits. Like the steady drip of water that carves canyons in solid rock, the consistent application of small practices in language learning has the power to reshape the contours of the mind, etching new linguistic pathways into the cerebral landscape. In the minutiae of daily routine, the seeds of multilingualism are sown, nurtured not by sporadic downpours of intensive study but by the gentle, persistent mist of habituation.

Daily Habits for Language Learning: Incorporating Small Practices

Integration into Routine

Imagine the morning ritual of brewing coffee, its aromas and rhythms a familiar comfort. Now, picture transforming this ritual into an immersive language lesson by labeling your coffee supplies in your target language. Depending on your linguistic focus, the coffee pot becomes la cafetera or die Kaffeemaschine. This simple yet effective practice turns a mundane activity into a fertile ground for learning, each morning brewing coffee and new vocabulary. The key lies in weaving language learning seamlessly into the fabric of daily life, transforming the ordinary into opportunities for practice and exposure.

Language Switch Days

Mark your calendar for days dedicated to living exclusively in your target language. From sunrise to sunset, immerse yourself in Spanish, French, Mandarin, or any language you're learning. These days, all tasks, from reading the news to jotting down shopping lists, are conducted in the chosen language. This immersion at home simulates the linguistic drench of living abroad, its challenges and triumphs compacted into the span of a day. The shift from one language to another enhances adaptability and deepens immersion; each switch day is a microcosm of linguistic dedication.

Tech Integration

In a world where technology is a constant companion, its potential as a tool for language learning is immense. Imagine your smartphone, a device often criticized for its distractions, transformed into an instrument of linguistic immersion. By changing your device's language settings, every interaction becomes a lesson. Navigating menus, responding to prompts, and even dealing with the occasional frustration when trying to find a particular setting—all these experiences reinforce familiarity with the language's structure and vocabulary. Furthermore, language learning apps offer structured practice during downtime, turning the wait at a bus stop or the line at a grocery store into moments ripe for learning.

Active Listening

Consider the soundtrack to your daily life—the music accompanying your morning routine, the podcasts filling your commutes. Now, imagine if this soundtrack were in your target language. By curating playlists of songs and subscribing to podcasts in the language you're learning, passive listening becomes an active tool for immersion. The melodies and rhythms of music make vocabulary memorable, while podcasts on topics of interest engage not just your linguistic skills but also your curiosity and intellect. This practice turns every melody heard, and every word listened to into threads woven into the tapestry of your linguistic competence.

Visual Element: Interactive Daily Habit Tracker

An interactive daily habit tracker is provided to support integrating these practices into your daily life. This digital tool allows you to log activities, from your morning coffee ritual in your target language to your evening podcast listening session. It offers reminders, encouragement, and progress tracking, turning the abstract goal of language learning into tangible, daily actions. The tracker serves as a record and a roadmap, guiding you through the landscape of daily habituation toward the destination of fluency.

In the confluence of these daily practices, language learning transcends the confines of classrooms and textbooks, spilling into everyday life. The habits formed in the quiet routine moments become the cornerstones of linguistic proficiency, each small practice a ripple expanding across the pond of knowledge. Through the deliberate integration of language into the minutiae of daily existence, the monumental task of learning multiple languages is rendered achievable and woven into the very fabric of daily life, each thread a testament to the power of persistence, immersion, and the transformative magic of routine.

The Role of Language in Identity: Living Through Your Languages

An intricate dance unfolds at the confluence of language and self, where identity is reflected and constructed through the multilingual mosaic of our linguistic repertoires. This subtle yet profound interplay shapes the essence of who we are, coloring our perceptions and expressions with the hues of the languages that resonate within us. To engage with multiple languages is, therefore, to navigate a landscape where each tongue weaves its thread into the fabric of our being, creating a tapestry rich with diversity and depth.

Personal Connection

In personal identity, each language is a mirror, reflecting facets of ourselves that might otherwise remain obscured. The intimacy of a mother tongue might evoke a sense of belonging, its words wrapping around us like a familial embrace. Conversely, a language acquired later in life might unlock doors to previously unexplored corridors of our identity, each new phrase a key to understanding aspects of our personality that thrive under the influence of different linguistic structures. This journey through language acquisition becomes a voyage of self-discovery, where learning is intertwined with the process of becoming. The nuances of each language, with its unique expressions of emotion and thought, offer new lenses through which to view the world and, by extension, ourselves.

The texture of our rich and multidimensional experiences adds layers to our identity, each language a brushstroke contributing to the evolving portrait of who we are.

Expression of Self

At any given moment, the choice of language is more than a matter of convenience or functionality; it is an act of self-expression, a declaration of identity. Conforming to one language over another is choosing the colors with which we paint our thoughts and feelings, selecting the palette that best captures the shades of our current emotional landscape. This selection might align with the cultural or familial heritage that a particular language evokes or might hinge on the expressive potential that another language offers for articulating a specific thought or sentiment. This fluidity in language choice allows for a dynamic expression of self, where multiple languages coalesce to form a multifaceted medium for personal expression. The interplay between these linguistic options enriches our communicative repertoire, enabling us to convey the complexity of our experiences and perspectives with a richness that transcends monolingual limitations.

Community Engagement

Learning a language invariably draws us into the orbit of its associated community, a gravitational pull that connects us to a network of speakers bound by shared linguistic ties. Participation in these communities, whether through cultural events, language exchange meetings, or online forums, deepens our connection to the language, rooting it in the lived experiences of its speakers. This immersion in the social fabric of a language not only enhances linguistic proficiency but also fosters a sense of belonging, of being part of a collective identity that transcends geographical and cultural boundaries. The language becomes a conduit for community engagement, a bridge linking us to the speakers' stories, traditions, and collective memory. Through this engagement, language acquisition transcends the realm of intellectual pursuit, becoming a means of cultural integration and social participation. The bonds formed in these linguistic communities enrich our understanding of the language, imbuing it with personal significance that anchors it firmly within the landscape of our identity.

Identity and Language Learning

Language learning trajectory is marked by moments of transformation, where the acquisition of new linguistic skills heralds a shift in self-perception and personal growth. Each language, with its unique worldview and expressive capabilities, offers a new mode of being, a different way of interacting with the world. This transformation is not merely additive, a simple expansion of linguistic repertoire, but metamorphic, altering the very fabric of our identity. The challenges encountered and overcome in the language learning process—moments of frustration, breakthrough, and connection—forge resilience, empathy, and open-mindedness. These experiences, woven into the narrative of our personal development, shape our linguistic abilities and character. The journey through multilingualism becomes a journey of self-reflection, where each language acts as a catalyst for personal evolution, challenging us to grow, adapt, and redefine ourselves in the context of an ever-expanding linguistic horizon.

In exploring the role of language in identity, we traverse the intimate landscape where self and language intersect, discovering how our linguistic journeys shape, reflect, and express who we are. This dance of identity and language, intricate and evolving, reveals the profound impact of multilingualism on our sense of self, highlighting the transformative power of language learning as a medium for personal expression, community engagement, and self-discovery. Through this lens, learning languages emerges as a deeply personal endeavor that enriches the tapestry of our identity with each new linguistic thread it introduces, crafting a portrait of self that is as diverse and dynamic as the languages that color its contours.

Multilingualism at Work: Leveraging Languages for Career Growth

In the winding corridors of the modern workplace, where the hum of global interconnectedness pulses through every interaction, the ability to navigate the multilingual tapestry of our professional environments emerges as a beacon of opportunity. In this context, the polyglot does not merely possess a skill but wields a key that unlocks doors to nuanced understandings, broadened perspectives, and, most critically, unparalleled career advancement.

Career Advantages

Navigating the competitive landscapes of today's job markets, the multilingual professional stands at the vanguard, a step removed from the monolingual majority. This linguistic skill confers distinct advantages, illuminating paths to roles that quickly demand the ability to overcome cross-cultural and linguistic barriers. In industries from international diplomacy to global finance and realms as diverse as technology startups and humanitarian NGOs, proficiency in multiple languages transcends the beneficial status—it becomes indispensable. More than a line on a resumé, it signals to potential employers a readiness for leadership in a world where boundaries blur, and markets merge. Multilingual individual, thus, do not simply advance within their chosen career; they redefine the parameters of possibility within it.

185

Language in Professional Settings

Integrating linguistic skills into professional settings demands more than casual proficiency; it requires a strategic, nuanced approach to communication. Consider, for instance, the preparation for a presentation to a multinational audience. Beyond the mere translation of slides, this entails adapting content to resonate across cultural landscapes, anticipating queries framed by diverse perspectives, and a delivery that balances linguistic accessibility with the sophistication expected in professional discourse. Similarly, in meetings where multiple languages ebb and flow, the ability to switch dialects, to paraphrase and summarize across linguistic divides, becomes a tool of engagement, fostering inclusivity and comprehension. In written communications, from emails to reports, clarity and cultural sensitivity in multilingual drafting avoid misinterpretations that could derail projects or relationships. Through these practices, language proficiency in professional settings becomes a means of communication and a strategy for leadership, diplomacy, and influence.

Networking

The realm of professional networking, too, is transformed under the influence of multilingual capabilities. Events, conferences, and social platforms present landscapes rich with potential connections, each interaction an opportunity to forge relationships that span the globe. The ability to converse in another's language breaks down barriers, creating moments of connection that transcend the transactional nature of professional networking. These interactions, whether in the corridors of a conference center or the comments of a LinkedIn post, lay the groundwork for collaborations, mentorships, and opportunities beyond the immediate horizon. Furthermore, networking in multiple languages cultivates a reputation as a connector and a professional capable of bridging worlds, thereby attracting opportunities from inaccessible spheres to those confined by linguistic limitations.

Continuous Improvement

Pursuing linguistic excellence in professional contexts is an endeavor marked by perpetual growth, a commitment to continuous improvement that mirrors the dynamism of the global market itself. This requires a proactive engagement with languages beyond the confines of necessity, seeking out opportunities for refinement and expansion. Subscribing to industry-specific publications in a target language, participating in professional forums, and attending workshops and seminars enhance proficiency and deepen industry knowledge. Engaging with experienced mentors who offer guidance in a target language provides insights into professional discourse, etiquette, and strategy nuances within different cultural contexts. Furthermore, the commitment to continuous improvement signals to employers and colleagues alike a dedication to excellence and adaptability, qualities that define the leaders of tomorrow's global workforce.

In this exploration of multilingualism in the workplace, we traverse the terrain of career advancement through the lens of linguistic diversity. From the strategic integration of language skills into professional practices to the cultivation of global networks and the commitment to ongoing linguistic and professional development, the multilingual individual emerges not just as a participant in the worldwide market but as a shaper of its future. Through this lens, language learning is recast as a career strategy, a deliberate cultivation of skills that propel individuals to the forefront of their fields, ready to navigate the complexities of a world where communication remains the cornerstone of success.

Language Learning with Family and Friends: A Collective Journey

Navigating the intricate landscapes of linguistic diversity often evokes the image of a solitary endeavor, a path tread in the quiet hours of introspection and study. Yet, woven into the fabric of this pursuit lies the potential for a shared voyage, where the contours of language and culture are explored not in isolation but in the company of those who form the bedrock of our social existence—family and friends. This collective expedition into multilingualism transforms the endeavor from a singular quest into a communal exploration, enriching the experience with the textures of shared discovery and mutual support.

Family Language Projects

In the sanctum of family life, where traditions are nurtured and bonds are forged, the introduction of language learning projects serves as a catalyst for collective growth. Imagine the creation of a family language tree, branches extending into the languages each member wishes to explore, roots anchored in the shared commitment to linguistic diversity. Each leaf on this tree represents a goal and a promise of shared effort and mutual encouragement. Engaging in such projects, families may allocate specific times for language-themed game nights or dedicate a portion of their evenings to story sessions in a chosen language. These activities, imbued with the warmth of familial connection, transcend mere language practice, embedding the learning process within the rituals of family life, making every word learned a testament to the collective endeavor and every mistake corrected a reflection of shared resilience.

Social Learning

Beyond the confines of family, extending language learning into friendship offers a vibrant arena for social learning. Here, creating language clubs or study groups among friends trans- forms the often-intimidating language acquisition process into an adventure to be shared. Picture a group of friends, each with unique linguistic aspirations, gathering in living rooms or cafes, their conversations a lively mosaic of languages being navigated with the buoyancy of camaraderie.

These sessions, whether focused on thematic discussions, language games, or collaborative learning exercises, harness the dynamic energy of friendship, channeling it into a force of linguistic expansion. Through laughter, encouragement, and the occasional good-natured ribbing, friends become co-navigators on the language learning journey, each bringing their unique strengths and perspectives to the collective endeavor.

Cultural Exchange Dinners

Breaking bread together has long been a symbol of communion and understanding, a ritual that transcends cultural and linguistic barriers. In multilingual learning, the organization of cultural exchange dinners elevates this ritual into a sensory-rich experience of linguistic and cultural immersion. Envision an evening where the flavors, sounds, and stories of a particular language's culture fill the air; each dish serves as a gateway to understanding and each conversation a bridge to linguistic insight. Through preparing and sharing meals representative of the languages being learned, participants embark on a culinary voyage where taste buds and linguistic faculties are engaged in equal measure. These gatherings, steeped in the aromas and tales of distant lands, offer a taste of the world's linguistic diversity, making the abstract tangibly delicious.

Support Systems

At the heart of this collective journey lies the creation of robust support systems, networks of encouragement, and accountability that sustain motivation and foster resilience. In this interconnected web of learners, each member becomes a pillar and a beneficiary, offering support when obstacles loom large and celebrating victories, no matter how small. Through regular check-ins, shared resources, and the mutual sharing of progress and challenges, these support systems operate as the lifeblood of the collective learning experience. They ensure that no learner walks alone, that every stumble is met with a helping hand, and that the chorus of communal celebration amplifies every achievement. This network, built on the foundations of trust, respect, and shared aspiration, becomes more than just a mechanism for language learning; it evolves into a community of practice, where the languages learned become threads in the larger tapestry of human connection.

In this shared odyssey of language learning with family and friends, the journey transcends the acquisition of linguistic proficiency, morphing into an exploration of the bonds that connect us, the cultures that enrich us, and the communal spirit that sustains us. Through family projects, social learning groups, cultural exchange dinners, and nurturing support systems, language learning is transformed from a solitary pursuit into a shared adventure, rich with the promise of discovery, the warmth of companionship, and the strength of collective endeavor. In this confluence of individual aspiration and communal support, language

191

learning becomes an avenue for personal growth and a bridge to deeper understanding and connection woven into our social existence.

The Art of Code-Switching: Navigating Multiple Languages Seamlessly

In the intricate dance of multilingual communication, code-switching emerges as a subtle yet richly nuanced performance. This linguistic phenomenon, where individuals alternate between languages within a single conversation or sentence, is not merely a matter of convenience or linguistic indecision. Instead, it is a testament to the cognitive agility and cultural adeptness of those who simultaneously inhabit more than one linguistic world. Code-switching is far from a linguistic aberration and a sophisticated skill reflecting the deeply intertwined nature of language, thought, and identity.

Understanding Code-Switching

At its core, code-switching is an innate response to the multifaceted demands of communication across linguistic boundaries. It unveils the capacity of the multilingual mind to navigate, with remarkable fluidity, the complex landscapes of language. This ability is not confined to vocabulary and grammar but extends into the subtleties of cultural nuance and contextual appropriateness. In essence, code-switching is the linguistic embodiment of adaptability, a bridge

192

constructed in real-time to span the chasms between diverse linguistic territories. For the multilingual individual, this phenomenon is not an anomaly but a natural aspect of linguistic repertoire, a tool wielded with precision to enhance communication, foster connection, and negotiate identity.

Practical Applications

The practical applications of code-switching extend far beyond the mechanics of language use, embedding themselves in the fabric of social interaction and cultural integration. In settings where multiple languages coalesce, code-switching becomes a dynamic instrument for achieving resonance with one's audience. It allows for the tailoring of messages to fit the linguistic comfort zones of interlocutors, thereby facilitating understanding and rapport. Moreover, in language learning, the strategic use of code-switching can serve as a scaffold, supporting the acquisition of new linguistic structures through the judicious incorporation of familiar elements. Blending the known with the unknown eases the cognitive load, making the unfamiliar more accessible and learning more fluid.

Code-Switching Etiquette

Navigating the social nuances of code-switching demands a keen awareness of the settings and cultures in which it occurs. The norms and expectations of the linguistic communities involved often dictate the appropriateness of code-switching. In some contexts, it may be celebrated as a display of linguistic proficiency and cultural empathy, while in others, it may be perceived as a breach of linguistic purity or a sign of disrespect. The multilingual communicator, therefore, must tread with sensitivity, attuned to the subtleties of social cues and cultural expectations. This sensitivity ensures that code-switching is employed not as a linguistic crutch but as a deliberate strategy for enhancing understanding, respecting cultural identities, and enriching the tapestry of communication.

Cognitive Benefits

The cognitive benefits of seamless language switching are manifold, highlighting the remarkable flexibility and resilience of the multilingual brain. Code-switching stimulates the brain's executive functions, particularly task-switching, attention, and inhibition. This constant juggling of linguistic systems sharpens cognitive control mechanisms and fortifies the neural networks responsible for language processing. Furthermore, code-switching fosters a heightened awareness of linguistic and cultural nuance, enriching the communicator's repertoire with various expressive possibilities. Within this intricate interplay of languages, the multilingual individual finds the capacity for linguistic adaptation and a deeper, more nuanced understanding of the human experience as expressed through language.

In code-switching, the multilingual communicator navigates a world where languages blend, boundaries blur, and meanings are negotiated in the crevices of cultural intersections. Far from being a linguistic no-man's-land, this realm is a vibrant space of creativity, innovation, and cognitive agility. Here, switching between languages is not just a matter of linguistic necessity but a celebration of the richness of human communication, a testament to the capacity of the multilingual mind to weave together disparate linguistic threads into a coherent, colorful tapestry of expression. In this dance of languages, the multilingual individual moves gracefully, each step reflecting the intricate, dynamic relationship between language, thought, and culture.

Cultural Immersion from Afar: Celebrating Multicultural Events

In the tapestry of multilingual education, threads of culture intertwine with linguistic strands, creating a fabric that envelops learners in the rich hues of global diversity. This fusion of language and culture transforms the endeavor from a mere academic pursuit into a vibrant foray into the lives and traditions of people across the globe. Within this context, celebrating multicultural events stands as a beacon, guiding learners toward immersive experiences that transcend physical boundaries, offering a taste of the world's vast cultural mosaic from the comfort of one's locale or digital screen.

Virtual Cultural Events

With its boundless capacity for connection, the digital age offers a portal into the heart of cultural festivities across continents. Virtual cultural events, webinars, and language exchange meetings serve as conduits, channeling the essence of far-flung celebrations into our living spaces. Engaging with these events, learners find themselves guests at a global table, where festivals unfold in real-time, webinars dissect the nuances of cultural practices, and language exchanges bloom into cross-cultural dialogues. While lacking the tangibility of physical presence, this virtual immersion compensates with accessibility and variety, allowing learners to traverse cultural landscapes with unprecedented ease. With each click a leap across borders, these digital encounters weave cultural understanding into the fabric of language learning, enriching the learner's arsenal with words and the breath of life that animates them.

Local Cultural Festivals

Yet, for those yearning for the tangible, the local sphere offers many opportunities to dive into the cultural dimensions of language. Cultural festivals and events, often nestled in the heart of communities, invite participation and exploration. Learners step into miniature representations of the world, where different cultures' sights, sounds, and scents converge. Engaging with these festivals, one navigates through stalls adorned with artifacts, savors dishes steeped in tradition, and sways to melodies that traverse linguistic barriers. These forays into local cultural celebrations serve as tactile lessons in diversity, where each interaction is a thread pulled from the global tapestry woven into the learners' understanding of the languages they seek to master. Through these experiences, the abstract becomes palpable, and language learning transcends the confines of textbooks, flourishing in the vibrant arena of human connection.

Cultural Cooking Nights

In the alchemy of the kitchen, where ingredients blend under the watchful eye of tradition, cultural cooking nights emerge as a celebration of culinary diversity. Organizing these gatherings, learners embark on gustatory voyages, where recipes act as maps, guiding them through the flavors of the languages they study. Each dish, from the simmering pots of a Thai curry to the meticulous assembly of a French pastry, tells a story, a narrative steeped in the history and practices of its people. These cooking nights, shared with family, friends, or fellow language enthusiasts, transform eating into an act of learning. The preparation process, often accompanied by discussions on the dish's cultural significance and linguistic roots, deepens the connection between language and the sensory experiences that define it. Here, language is spoken and tasted, its vocabulary infused in the aromas and textures of dishes that have traveled through time and space to find a place on the learner's table.

197

Cultural Arts and Crafts

Beyond the realm of taste lies the visual and tactile world of arts and crafts, a domain where culture manifests in form and color. Exploring the arts and crafts associated with different linguistic communities offers learners a hands-on approach to cultural understanding. Workshops on traditional painting techniques, craft sessions focused on indigenous textile patterns, or classes on the intricate art of calligraphy serve as gateways into the aesthetic expressions of culture. These activities, often requiring a delicate balance of attention and skill, mirror the complicated language-learning process. Each stroke of the brush, each weave of the fabric, parallels the construction of sentences, the shaping of sounds into words. Through the lens of arts and crafts, learners encounter the stories and values that underpin a culture, their hands shaping materials as their minds shape linguistic structures. This tactile engagement with culture serves as a reminder that language is not just a tool for communication but a living, breathing entity shaped by the hands and hearts of those who speak it.

In celebrating multicultural events, from the digital expanses of virtual gatherings to the tangible joys of local festivals, culinary adventures, and artistic explorations, learners immerse themselves in the rich tapestry of human culture. These experiences, bridging the gap between language and the lived reality of its speakers, illuminate the path to true linguistic proficiency—a path paved not just with words but with the tastes, sights, sounds, and textures of the diverse world we share. Through this immersion, language learners

198

do not merely acquire the tools of communication; they weave themselves into the ongoing story of cultural exchange, their learning journey a testament to the enduring power of human connection across the vast mosaic of global diversity.

Language Learning as a Lifestyle: Beyond the Classroom

Incorporating Language in Hobbies

The interweaving of linguistic pursuits with leisure activities offers a delightful confluence where passion meets practice, allowing for a seamless infusion of foreign words and phrases into the sanctuary of one's interests. Picture the avid reader whose shelves now brim with novels in multiple tongues, each page a voyage into the heart of another culture, every sentence a brushstroke on the canvas of their imagination. Similarly, envision gamers, controllers in hand, navigating virtual worlds where quests are undertaken and allies are made, all within the linguistic frameworks they aspire to master. This synthesis transforms hobbies into fertile grounds for linguistic growth, ensuring that language acquisition transcends the boundaries of obligation and becomes intertwined with the threads of personal joy and curiosity. Through this melding, hobbies become more than mere pastimes; they evolve into vibrant classrooms without walls, where the engine of intrinsic motivation powers learning.

Travel as Education

The act of traversing the globe, once seen merely as an escape from the mundane, now reveals its true potential as a profound educational tool, a means through which the theoretical becomes tangible. In this light, travel sheds its leisurely skin to emerge as an immersive classroom, its lessons inscribed in the streets of bustling cities, whispered by the winds of ancient ruins and reflected in the eyes of those who call those distant lands home. This perspective transforms each journey into a meticulously crafted lesson in language and culture, where every interaction is a dialogue, every sign a text to be deciphered, and every cultural nuance a puzzle to be solved. Through the lens of linguistic curiosity, travelers become not mere tourists, but students of the world; their sojourns are a series of immersive tutorials in the art of communication and understanding. This approach to travel, marked by an insatiable appetite for linguistic and cultural immersion, ensures that every destination becomes a milestone in the language acquisition journey, a tangible reminder of the world's vast linguistic tapestry.

Lifelong Learning Mindset

Adopting a perspective that views language learning not as a finite goal but as a perpetual endeavor marks a pivotal shift in the narrative of linguistic acquisition. This mindset, rooted in recognizing that language is a living entity, constantly evolving and expanding, invites learners to embrace the fluidity of their linguistic journey. It acknowledges that mastery is not a destination but a horizon, always within sight yet forever extending as one advances. This ethos encourages learners to revel in the learning process, find satisfaction in incremental progress, and remain open to the endless possibilities of linguistic exploration. It fosters an environment where curiosity is the compass that guides one's path, and resilience is the wind that propels one forward. Within this framework, language learning becomes a vibrant thread woven into the fabric of one's life, a continuous pursuit that enriches every moment with the potential for discovery and growth.

Community Involvement

Engagement with linguistic and cultural communities, both within the physical embrace of one's locale and the boundless realms of the digital world, offers a rich tapestry of opportunities for practice, exchange, and growth. This involvement, whether in the participation in local language meetups, the contribution to online forums, or the attendance at cultural festivals, serves as a vital lifeline, connecting learners to a network of like-minded individuals. It transforms the often solitary act of language learning into a communal experience where challenges are shared, achievements celebrated, and knowledge freely exchanged. Through active participation in these communities, learners hone their linguistic skills and deepen their cultural understanding, forging connections that transcend linguistic barriers.

This engagement, powered by the collective energy of community, becomes a wellspring of motivation, a source of inspiration and support that sustains learners throughout their journey. In the crucible of community, language learning transcends the confines of individual endeavor to become a shared journey, a collaborative quest to pursue linguistic and cultural fluency.

In this exploration of language learning as a lifestyle, the journey unfolds not within the four walls of a classroom but in the expansive arena of life itself. It is a path marked by the joyful merging of hobbies with linguistic growth, the transformative power of travel, the enduring commitment to lifelong learning, and the vibrant engagement with the community. Through this holistic approach, language acquisition becomes not just an educational goal but a way of life, a continuous journey woven into the very essence of one's daily existence. In this narrative, every book, every game, every journey, and every community interaction becomes a chapter in the story of linguistic growth, a testament to the boundless potential for learning that lies in the fabric of everyday life.

Lifelong Language Learning: Strategies for Keeping Languages Alive

Regular engagement with the languages one seeks to retain is akin to tending a garden; it requires consistent care, strategic nourishment, and a keen awareness of the evolving needs of each linguistic plant in one's mental landscape. Establishing routines incorporating even the smallest doses of language practice ensures the roots remain robust and the foliage vibrant. This can manifest in myriad forms, such as setting aside moments each morning to review a handful of new words, integrating language apps into the brief pauses that punctuate the day, or dedicating evening hours to the pleasure of a film or book in the target language. Though gentle, the cadence of this practice beats a steady rhythm that keeps the language alive in the consciousness, allowing fluency to flourish even in the face of time's relentless march.

Setting advanced learning goals acts as a beacon, illuminating the path forward and directing the language learning odyssey. These objectives should stretch the learner, pushing the boundaries of comfort and familiarity to reach new linguistic heights. Whether aspiring to read a complex novel, deliver a speech, or comprehend the nuances of a foreign film without subtitles, these ambitions serve as milestones, marking progress and fueling motivation. The journey toward these goals, fraught with challenges and adorned with victories, imbues the process with a sense of purpose, transforming the routine into a quest for linguistic mastery.

Sharing one's linguistic knowledge with others, stepping into the role of mentor or tutor, illuminates the path for fellow learners and casts a reflective light on one's understanding. In articulating language concepts to one another, the intricacies of grammar, vocabulary, and pronunciation are clarified, solidifying the mentor's grasp of the language. This reciprocal exchange, where teaching becomes a tool for learning, enriches both participants, weaving a more robust fabric of comprehension and capability. The mentorship journey, packed with the exchange of knowledge and the mutual discovery of linguistic landscapes, fosters a deeper connection to the language, reinforcing its presence in the mind and heart.

Continuous exposure to the target language through media, literature, conversation, and travel ensures that the language remains a living, breathing entity within one's daily existence. Immersing oneself in the harmonious flow of a language, whether through the whispered pages of a book, the vibrant dialogue of a movie, the dynamic exchange of conversation, or the immersive experience of travel, keeps the linguistic waters stirring. This exposure, rich and varied, feeds the roots of fluency, allowing it to deepen and spread. In absorbing language through these channels, learners find themselves enveloped in a linguistic cocoon, from which they emerge, time and again, transformed by the richness of expression and the depth of cultural insight gained.

Exploring strategies for sustaining and nurturing language proficiency over a lifetime, we discover methods and a manifesto for linguistic engagement. From the rhythmic cadence of regular practice to the aspirational beacon of advanced learning goals, the enriching cycle of mentorship, and the vibrant tapestry of continuous exposure, each element contributes to a comprehensive strategy for keeping languages vibrant and alive. This approach, rooted in commitment, curiosity, and connection, ensures that the languages we choose to learn become integral threads in the fabric of our lives, coloring our perceptions, shaping our interactions, and enriching our understanding of the world.

As we close this section, let us hold fast to the understanding that language, in its essence, is more than a tool for communication; it is a medium for connection, a pathway to learning, and a key to unlocking the vast treasures of human culture and knowledge. The strategies outlined here guide us to weave language into the essence of our being and approach the lifelong language learning journey with a spirit of exploration, openness, and joy. With these principles as our compass, we move forward, ever eager to discover the next horizon, embrace the next challenge, and deepen our engagement with the rich tapestry of human language that binds us all.

9

Chapter 8: Navigating the Future of Language Learning

In the evolving language education landscape, the quiet hum of innovation whispers promises of transformation. This revolution, powered by technology, reshapes how languages are learned, broadening horizons and dismantling barriers with the vigor of a relentless tide. Consider the moment the first book was printed; it must have felt like an unveiling of knowledge to the masses. Today, we stand at a similar cusp, where technology redefines access, personalization, and connection in language learning, offering tools that adapt to our linguistic needs and the nuances of our learning patterns.

The Evolution of Language Learning Technologies: What's Next?

Technological Advancements

In recent years, we have witnessed an unparalleled surge in technological innovations to refine the language acquisition process. From sophisticated apps that leverage spaced repetition algorithms to virtual classrooms that connect learners across continents, the arsenal of tools at the disposal of language learners expands with each passing day. Predicting future trends, we see the bright horizon with the promise of technologies that streamline learning and make it more immersive. Imagine a world where augmented reality overlays provide real-time translations and cultural insights as you navigate a foreign city, turning every street corner into a lesson in language and culture.

Personalized Learning

At the heart of these technological advancements lies the power of artificial intelligence (AI) to craft learning experiences that adapt to the individual. Once a lofty ideal, personalized learning is rapidly becoming a tangible reality. AI algorithms analyze learners' performance, preferences, and pace, tailoring content to fit their unique learning trajectories. This approach mirrors the experience of having a personal tutor who understands your strengths and challenges and guides you through the language learning process with precision. The shift towards personalized learning promises a future where frustration and stagnation give way to progress and enthusiasm, where learners no longer feel lost in a sea of generic content.

Accessibility

Technology stands as a great equalizer in the realm of education, and language learning is no exception. Innovations in language learning technologies have made resources more accessible to people worldwide, regardless of geography, economic status, or physical ability. Language apps, online courses, and digital textbooks provided unimaginable learning opportunities just a few decades ago. This democratization of language education opens doors for millions to learn new languages, bridging gaps and fostering understanding in an increasingly interconnected world.

Community and Connection

The digital age has redefined the concept of community, extending its boundaries beyond physical spaces to encompass global networks of learners. Online platforms and language learning forums offer spaces where individuals can share insights, ask questions, and find language partners. These communities, vibrant with a shared passion for languages, offer support and motivation, turning the language learning process into a collective endeavor. The importance of these online communities is set to grow, transforming language learning from a solitary pursuit into a shared journey enriched by the diversity and camaraderie of learners from around the globe.

Visual Element: Interactive Language Learning Technology Timeline

To illustrate the rapid evolution of language learning technologies, an interactive timeline charts the journey from traditional textbooks to the cutting-edge AI-driven tools of today. This visual element, accessible online, invites users to explore each milestone, offering insights into the innovations that have shaped language education over the years. With each click, users uncover the stories behind the technologies, understanding how they work and how they revolutionize how we learn languages.

This exploration of the future of language learning technologies unveils a landscape where innovation, personalization, accessibility, and community converge to create engaging, effective, and inclusive learning experiences. As we navigate this landscape, we are reminded that at the core of every technological advancement lies the timeless pursuit of knowledge and connection, a quest that technology not only facilitates but also enriches, opening new pathways to understanding and bridging the divides between us.

The Role of Artificial Intelligence in Language Acquisition

In the labyrinth of language acquisition, artificial intelligence (AI) emerges as both the Minotaur and the thread of Ariadne, presenting challenges that spur innovation while simultaneously providing solutions that guide learners through the maze of linguistic complexity. This duality encapsulates the essence of AI's role in modern language learning— a force that continuously reshapes the educational landscape through its ability to personalize, adapt, and engage.

AI Tutors

The advent of AI-driven tutors marks a paradigm shift in personalized language instruction. These digital mentors, with their capacity for infinite patience and their absence of judg- ment, offer a learning experience that is both nurturing and efficient. Unlike their human counterparts, AI tutors are not constrained by time, allowing for an instructional model that accommodates the learner's pace, encouraging exploration and minimizing the fear of failure. This environment fosters a deeper engagement with the language as learners interact with AI tutors who dynamically adjust teaching strategies based on real-time feedback. The dialogue with an AI tutor evolves into a dance, where steps are neither led nor followed but emerge from the harmony of algorithmic insight and human curiosity.

Speech Recognition

Using speech recognition technology in language learning tools bridges the silent comprehension of written text and the vibrant world of spoken communication. This technology listens with an unbiased ear, offering corrections and suggestions that refine pronunciation and enhance listening skills. Learners find themselves in a responsive auditory landscape, where nuances of accent, intonation, and rhythm are not merely observed but actively sculpted. The feedback loop created by speech recognition technology accelerates the acquisition of speaking and listening skills, transforming solitary utterances into dialogues with an unseen, attentive speaker.

Content Customization

At the intersection of AI and language learning lies the power of content customization— a dynamic process where learning materials evolve in response to the learner's progress and preferences. This adaptive content generation ensures that the learner's journey through language acquisition is paved with materials that challenge without overwhelming, facilitating a steady ascent towards proficiency. The AI's ability to analyze performance data and predict learning needs allows for creating a curriculum as unique as the fingerprint of the learner's mind. This personalized approach ensures that every exercise, reading passage, and quiz is a building block strategically placed to support the learner's growth, making the path to language mastery a construct of their achievements and aspirations.

Language Learning Games

In AI-powered language learning games, education, and entertainment converge, creating an engaging and effective platform for linguistic development. With their roots in the fertile ground of AI algorithms, these games adapt to the player's language level, offering challenges that skillfully balance the edge of competence with the precipice of complexity. Through quests, puzzles, and interactive stories, learners are drawn into narratives that require linguistic skills to navigate, turning the act of language acquisition into an adventure. The immersive nature of these games captivates the learner's attention, harnessing the innate human love for play in the service of education. Each victory within the game becomes a step towards language proficiency, embedding vocabulary and grammar into the learner's mind through the memorable medium of play.

In this exploration of the role of artificial intelligence in language acquisition, we witness the transformation of learning from a static transfer of knowledge into a dynamic journey of discovery. With its dual capacity as a tutor and tool, AI offers a bridge across the chasm of language learning, making the trip possible and pleasurable. Through the personalized guidance of AI tutors, the corrective lens of speech recognition, the adaptive landscapes of customized content, and the engaging realms of language learning games, AI shapes a future where language education is accessible, effective, and deeply engaging. In this future, the path to language mastery is not a solitary trek through uncharted territory but a guided exploration of a world rich with the sounds and symbols of human expression facilitated by the intelligent hand of technology.

Virtual Reality and Language Learning: Immersive Experiences

In the realm where digital innovation converges with the pursuit of linguistic proficiency, virtual reality (VR) emerges as a pivotal force, reshaping the contours of traditional language education. This technology, once relegated to the domains of gaming and entertainment, now reveals its profound potential in crafting immersive language learning environments. These digital realms offer learners an unparalleled opportunity to simulate real-life interactions and scenarios, transcending the limitations of physical classrooms and static textbooks. In these meticulously designed virtual spaces, learners find themselves navigating through bustling market streets, engaging in dialogue with native speakers, and absorbing cultural nuances, all within the safety and comfort of their learning sanctuary.

The leap into VR-assisted language learning extends beyond mere novelty; it represents a fundamental shift toward experiential education. Within these immersive environments, a new language's abstract symbols and sounds gain tangible form, allowing learners to interact with them as naturally as they would in the physical world. Imagine ordering food in a Parisian café, with each exchange, from reading the menu to conversing with the waiter, serving as an authentic practice of language skills. Such scenarios, replicated with remarkable fidelity in VR, bridge the gap between theoretical knowledge and practical application, fostering a deep, experiential understanding of the language.

Moreover, the potential of VR to envelop learners in rich cultural tapestries offers an avenue for cultural immersion that traditional methodologies struggle to match. Beyond the mastery of syntax and vocabulary, language learning is intrinsically linked to understanding the cultural context from which it springs. Herein lies the transformative power of VR: to transport learners to the heart of cultural festivals, the solemnity of traditional ceremonies, or the vibrancy of everyday life across the globe. This immersion in the cultural dimensions of language learning enriches the educational experience and cultivates empathy and global awareness, traits indispensable in our interconnected world.

The interactive learning opportunities presented by VR technology starkly contrast conventional educational approaches. Through hands-on experiences facilitated by VR, learners actively participate in their education, applying language skills in real-time and making decision-making scenarios that mimic life's unpredictability. This active engagement fosters a sense of agency in learners, encouraging exploration and experimentation within a safe, controlled environment. The immediate feedback provided by interactive VR experiences aids in rapidly adjusting and refining language skills, accelerating the journey toward fluency.

Despite its promise, the widespread adoption of VR in language education faces challenges, particularly regarding accessibility and scalability. Though decreasing, VR technology's cost and complexity remain prohibitive for many, limiting the reach of these innovative learning experiences. Furthermore, the development of high-quality, pedagogically sound VR content demands a significant investment of resources, from linguistic expertise to technical prowess. Addressing these challenges necessitates a collaborative approach involving educators, technologists, and policymakers in concerted efforts to democratize access to VR language learning tools.

Efforts to expand the accessibility of VR language learning tools have begun to take shape, with initiatives aimed at reducing costs and simplifying technology. Open-source platforms and community-driven content creation are promising avenues for bringing immersive language learning experiences to a broader audience. Additionally, the scalability of VR-based education benefits from advances in cloud computing and the development of lightweight, affordable VR hardware, paving the way for more learners to explore virtual reality's linguistic and cultural landscapes.

The integration of VR technology into language education heralds a new era of immersive learning, where the boundaries between learner and environment, between language and culture, blur into a cohesive, engaging educational experience. Through immersive environments, cultural immersion, interactive learning, and efforts to

215

enhance accessibility and scalability, VR stands poised to redefine the landscape of language education. In doing so, it offers learners a new tool for language acquisition and a portal to the world, inviting them to step through and discover the rich tapestry of human communication and connection.

The Future of Language Exchange: Global Connections

In the tapestry of modern language learning, the threads of digital platforms weave intricate patterns of global connections, revolutionizing traditional paradigms of linguistic exchange. This new era, characterized by the seamless intertwining of cultures and languages, owes its vibrancy to the proliferation of online platforms that foster linguistic partnerships across continents. Within these digital realms, barriers of distance and time dissolve, allowing for the spontaneous combustion of cultural and linguistic exchanges that enrich both participants. The democratization of language learning through these platforms heralds a shift towards a more inclusive, accessible education model, where the only passport required is curiosity and the willingness to engage.

Navigating these platforms, one discovers a world where language learners and native speakers converge, each seeking to offer and gain linguistic insights. This symbiotic relationship, facilitated by the intuitive interfaces of apps and websites, transcends the conventional student-teacher dynamic, fostering instead a community of equals united by mutual goals. The beauty of this approach lies in its simplicity and profound impact on breaking down linguistic and cultural barriers. Through regular interactions, learners gain fluency and an intimate understanding of the cultural subtleties that animate language, transforming every conversation into a bridge that connects disparate worlds.

Once confined to the physical act of travel, the essence of cultural exchange now finds expression in the virtual interactions facilitated by language learning platforms. Though mediated by screens, these interactions pulse with the warmth of genuine connection, offering glimpses into the lives and traditions of people worlds apart. The ease with which learners can now immerse themselves in a language's cultural context without leaving their homes is revolutionary. It is a testament to the power of technology to bring the world closer, making the rich tapestry of global cultures more accessible to those who seek to understand and appreciate them.

Peer learning methodologies, reimagined in the digital age, reflect a profound understanding of the collaborative nature of language acquisition. Innovations in this area leverage language learners' collective knowledge and experience, creating learning ecosystems where insights are shared, challenges are collectively tackled, and successes are celebrated. This collaborative model, underscored by the principles of reciprocity and mutual respect, fosters an environment where learning is not just a solitary pursuit but a communal journey. The peer-to-peer approach encourages learners to step into the role of both student and teacher, deepening their understanding of the language while contributing to the growth of others.

This methodology, facilitated by technology, mirrors how languages are learned and used in real life, making the learning process more dynamic, engaging, and effective.

The role of language exchange in building global networks and communities cannot be overstated. Each learner is a node and a connector in this interconnected web, linked by the common thread of linguistic curiosity. The networks formed through language exchange platforms extend beyond the confines of language learning, fostering professional connections, friendships, and a profound sense of global belonging. This worldwide network, characterized by diversity and inclusivity, is a beacon of what can be achieved when communication barriers are dismantled. The communities that emerge from these interactions are vibrant ecosystems of cultural exchange, where languages serve not only as tools for communication but as bridges to understanding.

In this landscape, the future of language exchange shines brightly, illuminated by the potential for deeper cultural understanding, innovative learning methodologies, and the formation of global networks. The evolution of digital platforms continues redefining the possibilities for language exchange, promising a future where learning languages is not just about acquiring fluency but about connecting with the world meaningfully. In this future, the richness of human connection, facilitated by the exchange of languages and cultures, offers a powerful antidote to the divisions that fragment our world, weaving a tapestry of unity from the threads of diversity.

Maintaining Multiple Languages: Strategies for Long-term Success

A delicate balance must be struck in the realm where linguistic diversity flourishes, for the multilingual mind, thrives not on stagnant pools of knowledge but on the flowing rivers of continuous practice and engagement. The task of nurturing proficiency in several tongues demands a nuanced understanding of the dynamics of language retention, a comprehension that transcends mere acquisition to embrace the complexities of maintenance. This intricate dance, performed on the stage of the polyglot's mind, requires a choreography that melds discipline with creativity and structure with spontaneity, ensuring that each language remains a living, breathing entity within the cognitive landscape.

Continuous Learning

Pursuing perpetual growth in multiple languages unfolds as an odyssey through uncharted territories, where the familiar shores of initial fluency recede, revealing the vast expanses of advanced proficiency. This journey demands the navigator's skill and a vessel equipped for the voyage—a repertoire of strategies designed for the deep waters of ongoing linguistic development. At the core of these strategies lies the principle of immersion, a deliberate plunge into environments where language lives not as a subject of study but as a medium of life. This immersion might manifest in daily habits, where the languages in question serve as the lens through which the world is experienced, from the morning news consumed in one tongue to the evening's leisure reading in another. Additionally, engaging with content that challenges—through sophisticated literature, technical articles, or philosophical discourses—ensures that the mind remains a battleground where linguistic skills are honed and sharpened.

Advanced Studies

For those who seek not just to maintain but to elevate their linguistic prowess, the path of advanced studies beckons, offering avenues for deep exploration and specialized mastery. This path might traverse the halls of academia, where courses and degrees in foreign languages provide structured environments for rigorous study, or it might wind through the less formal but equally enriching landscapes of workshops, webinars, and online courses focused on specific aspects of language use. Beyond the academic, immersion experiences stand as pillars of advanced linguistic development, where time spent in regions where the target languages are spoken provides a crucible for transforming theoretical knowledge into practical skill. These experiences, rich with the textures of direct interaction and cultural engagement, serve not only to reinforce existing linguistic abilities but also to expand them, pushing the boundaries of fluency into the realms of nuanced, sophisticated expression.

Professional Use

The tapestry of professional life offers a fertile ground for the practical application and maintenance of multiple languages. In this arena, multilingualism transforms from an abstract asset into a tangible tool, wielded with precision to navigate the complexities of international business, diplomacy, and global collaboration. Integrating language skills into professional contexts might unfold through presentations conducted in a foreign tongue, negotiations that traverse linguistic divides, or the drafting of reports that cater to a diverse audience. Moreover, the professional environment serves as a continuous feedback loop, where the efficacy of communication directly influences outcomes, providing a powerful incentive for ongoing language improvement. This skilled use of language, underpinned by the need for accuracy, clarity, and cultural sensitivity, propels learners into continuous learning, where each task becomes a lesson, each challenge a test of linguistic agility.

Cultural Engagement

At the intersection of language and culture lies the heart of accurate linguistic maintenance—a relationship that feeds not only on the mechanics of grammar and vocabulary but on the rich tapestry of human expression and experience. Cultural engagement, therefore, emerges as a critical component of language retention, a dynamic interaction that infuses language learning with relevance and vitality. This engagement might take myriad forms, from participation in cultural festivals and events that celebrate the traditions of the language's native speakers to the exploration of art, film, music, and cuisine that embody the soul of the culture. Each of these interactions serves as a thread, binding the learner more closely to the language by grounding it in the lived reality of its use. Through cultural engagement, language transcends the confines of utility to become a bridge to understanding, a conduit through which the shared humanity of diverse peoples is explored and celebrated.

In the delicate art of maintaining proficiency in multiple languages, the polyglot navigates a landscape rich with challenges and rewards. In this terrain, growth is measured not in the accumulation of words but in the depth of understanding and the breadth of connection. This journey, marked by continuous learning, advanced studies, professional use, and cultural engagement, unfolds as a testament to the enduring power of language to connect, enrich, and transform. Its pursuit of linguistic diversity is a journey that celebrates the profound complexity and beauty of human communication.

The Impact of Multilingualism on Global Citizenship

In the intricate web of modern global society, the ability to communicate across the myriad cultural and linguistic divides is not merely an asset; it is a conduit through which empathy, understanding, and unity are fostered.

Multilingualism is at the heart of this dynamic interplay, a beacon guiding humanity toward a more cohesive existence. Through the lens of cross-cultural understanding, nurturing multilingual abilities illuminates paths to empathy previously shadowed by linguistic barriers. This illumination reveals not just the words of foreign tongues but the souls of the cultures they represent, allowing for a connection that transcends verbal communication. In the hands of individuals fluent in the world's languages, every conversation becomes a bridge, and every exchange is a step toward mutual respect and understanding.

The role of multilingual individuals in addressing global challenges emerges with pronounced significance in a world increasingly characterized by interdependence. Complex issues that span borders—from climate change to political unrest— demand a collective approach predicated on the ability to negotiate, collaborate, and empathize across cultural lines. The multilingual communicator navigates these waters with the advantage of perspective, their linguistic skills enabling not just the sharing of information but the sharing of viewpoints, fostering collaborative solutions that draw on the diverse strengths of global communities. This collaborative potential, unlocked by the keys of language, positions multilingual indi- viduals as architects of global problem-solving, their linguistic dexterity complementing their capacity for innovation and cooperation.

Amidst the vibrant tapestry of human culture, language is a testament to our collective heritage's rich diversity. In this context, the pursuit of language learning acquires a dimension of cultural preservation, safeguarding the voices of minority communities whose languages teeter on the brink of silence. For every individual who chooses to learn a language not just for communication but for connection, the act becomes one of preservation, an affirmation of the value of linguistic diversity in the grand mosaic of human existence. This dedication to preserving endangered languages and cultures adds depth to language learning, transforming it from a personal pursuit into a collective act of cultural conservation. The significance of this endeavor echoes through generations, ensuring that the voices of the past continue to resonate in the future, their wisdom, stories, and identities preserved in the living archive of language.

The development of global identity through multilingualism reflects a profound shift in self-perception, reimagining the individual not as a solitary entity defined by a single culture but as a node in the expansive network of global humanity. This identity, forged in the crucible of linguistic diversity, embraces the complexity of the human experience, recognizing the shared threads that bind us across cultural and linguistic divides. The implications of this shift for future generations are profound, promising a world where understanding and cooperation are the cornerstones of global society. Through the lens of multilingualism, individuals see not just the diversity of the world but its unity, their languages serving not as barriers but as keys to unlocking the full spectrum of human potential. This vision of a global identity, rooted in the principles of empathy, understanding, and cooperation, offers a blueprint for a future where the challenges of the world are met not with division but with unity, not with isolation but with the collective strength of humanity united by the bonds of language.

In this exploration of the impact of multilingualism on global citizenship, we uncover the threads that link language to empathy, collaboration, cultural preservation, and the cultivation of an international identity. Through this intricate web of connections, language emerges not just as a tool for communication but as a foundation for a more connected, understanding, and unified world. Multilingualism, in its capacity to bridge divides and illuminate commonalities, is a beacon guiding humanity toward a future characterized by empathy and collaboration, where the diverse tapestry of human culture is celebrated and preserved for generations to come.

Beyond Fluency: Achieving Proficiency in Multiple Languages

In the realm where words are both the currency and the fabric of our social tapestry, achieving proficiency transcends the mere accumulation of vocabulary and grammatical rules. It beckons the learner into the depths where cultural nuances breathe life into the skeleton of language, where idiomatic expressions and subtle linguistic cues paint vivid landscapes of meaning. This pursuit of proficiency is not a linear path but a spiraling ascent, demanding dedication and a nuanced understanding of the multifaceted nature of language itself.

Navigating this terrain requires a map that charts not the geography of language but its soul. In this exploration, one discovers the essence of proficiency—a command over language that allows for the articulation of complex ideas, easy navigation of social contexts, and a deep appreciation for the cultural underpinnings that shape linguistic expression. This mastery goes beyond fluency; it is the ability to wield language with the precision of a craftsman, shaping thoughts and ideas with the tools of words, tenses, and tones, crafting messages that resonate with clarity and depth.

Strategies for cultivating these advanced language skills hinge on immersion and deliberate practice. In this context, immersion is not merely a physical relocation but an intellectual and emotional engagement with the language. It involves surrounding oneself with the music of the language, its literature, media, and conversations, allowing the rhythm and flow of its expressions to seep into one's consciousness. On the other hand, deliberate practice is the conscious effort to refine and expand one's command over the language. It involves challenging oneself with complex texts, engaging in discussions on intricate topics, and writing with intent and purpose. This combination of immersion and deliberate practice paves the way for a profound understanding of the language and its cultural context, a prerequisite for true proficiency.

Applying multiple languages in professional and academic spheres adds another layer to the quest for proficiency. Here, language is not just a medium of communication but a tool for persuasion, negotiation, and disseminating knowledge. In academic contexts, it involves engaging with scholarly works, contributing to academic discourse, and navigating the intricacies of specialized terminology. In professional environments, it translates to the capacity to collaborate with international teams, understand and respect cultural differences in business practices, and communicate effectively in diverse settings. Achieving this level of proficiency demands an acute awareness of the nuances of language as it is used in specific contexts, an understanding cultivated through exposure, experience, and an unyielding commitment to learning.

Viewing language proficiency as a lifelong journey acknowledges the ever-evolving nature of language and our relationship with it. It is an admission that mastery is not a final destination but a perpetual horizon, always within sight yet forever receding as we advance. This perspective fosters a mindset of continuous learning, where each conversation, each book, and each interaction is an opportunity to refine and expand one's linguistic repertoire. It is a journey marked by milestones of understanding, each a testament to the depth of one's engagement with the language and its cultural essence.

In this ceaseless pursuit, the legacy of language becomes not the words we master but the bridges we build. It is a legacy that transcends the individual, inspiring the next generation of polyglots to not only reach for fluency but to delve deeper, seeking the profound connection that comes with true proficiency. This legacy is not measured in vocabulary or grammar but in the understanding and empathy that flourish when we genuinely comprehend not just the words of another language but its heart.

Therefore, proficiency in multiple languages is more than an academic or professional endeavor; it is a commitment to understanding the world's linguistic diversity. It is a vow to speak and listen, not just to articulate but to comprehend. In this commitment lies the essence of global citizenship, a recognition of the power of language to connect us, expand our perspectives, and enrich our understanding of the human experience.

Creating a Legacy of Language: Inspiring the Next Generation of Polyglots

In the mosaic of human achievement, the nurturing of linguistic diversity occupies a central tableau, its colors vibrant with the potential to shape minds, bridge cultures, and open doors to unexplored worlds. Within this context, disseminating personal narratives and successes transcends mere storytelling, serving instead as a beacon that illuminates the path for those who aspire to join the ranks of polyglots. Each tale of linguistic conquest, replete with its trials, triumphs, and transformative power, sews seeds of inspiration in fertile minds, compelling them to pursue the richness of multilingualism. These stories shared through forums, blogs, and social media or whispered in the ears of eager learners, carry the weight of possibility, painting a picture of a world made smaller and more intimate through the power of language.

The advocacy for language education emerges as a clarion call to action, a rallying cry that seeks to elevate the importance of multilingualism within educational systems and communities.

This activism, grounded in the conviction that language learning is not a luxury but a necessity in our interconnected world, drives efforts to infuse curricula with the tools and resources necessary to cultivate linguistic skills. Armed with data on multilingualism's cognitive, cultural, and economic benefits, advocates engage policymakers, educators, and parents in a dialogue to reshape educational priorities, ensuring that language learning occupies a central place in forming future global citizens.

Mentorship, in its most profound sense, serves as the bridge that connects experienced polyglots with those just beginning their linguistic journeys. This guidance, generous in its knowledge sharing and rich with the wisdom of experience, offers a lifeline to learners navigating the complexities of multiple languages. Through their encouragement, insight, and shared passion, mentors light the way, easing the isolation that can accompany intensive language study. Their presence, as a constant reminder of the tangible achievements that dedication and perseverance can yield, fosters a sense of community and belonging among language learners, reinforcing the notion that the pursuit of multilingualism is a journey best undertaken with companions.

Cultural exchange programs embody language learning's ultimate goal: fostering understanding and connection across the chasms that divide us. Whether physical or virtual, participation in these exchanges offers learners an immersive experience that transcends language acquisition to touch the heart of cultural discovery. Through the lived experience of another culture, language learners gain fluency and a deep appreciation for the diversity of human expression, tradition, and thought. By bringing together individuals from disparate backgrounds to share, learn, and grow, these programs act as powerful catalysts for developing empathy, respect, and a profound global interconnectedness.

In this endeavor to forge a legacy of language, the collective efforts to inspire, advocate, mentor, and exchange are not merely activities but acts of creation, contributing to a world where barriers to understanding are dismantled, one word, one conversation, one connection at a time. Through these efforts, the next generation of polyglots is nurtured, equipped not only with the ability to speak multiple languages but also with the vision to see the world through the eyes of others. This legacy, rooted in the power of language to unite and empower, stands as a testament to the potential within each of us to contribute to a more connected, empathetic, and understanding world.

As we reflect on the journey through the landscapes of multilingualism, the lessons learned, the insights gained, and the connections forged offer a map for those who follow. This exploration, rich with the promise of discovery and the joy of communication, beckons us forward, inviting us to continue our exploration of language, culture, and connection. The path ahead, illuminated by the legacy we create today, leads us into a world where the voices of many speak as one, celebrating the diversity and unity of the human experience.

10

Conclusion

Hey there, fellow language enthusiast! We've been through quite the journey together, haven't we? From those first baby steps of understanding the cognitive whirlwind that multilingualism brings into our lives to weaving these new languages into the fabric of our daily routines for that sweet, sweet taste of success, it's been nothing short of transformative, and I hope you've felt that spark of excitement and discovery on every page.

Remember how we discussed the importance of a custom fit when learning languages? Like a bespoke suit or a tailor-made dress, your language-learning journey should be cut and stitched to fit you perfectly. Our strategies must wrap around your brain, time, and dreams snugly and efficiently. There's no one-size-fits-all here. Your path is yours alone, crafted from your unique mix of cognitive styles, life's rhythms, and those big, bright goals you're reaching for.

We've unpacked a treasure chest of strategies together, haven't we? From turning your daily routines into multilingual gold mines to leveraging the latest tech to keep you on track, we've covered ground that will serve you well on this journey. And let's not forget the incredible lifelong perks of being a polyglot—boosted brain power, deeper cultural connections, and opening doors to global adventures. These aren't just nice-to-haves; they're tangible benefits that can enrich your life in ways you've yet to imagine.

So, here's where I nudge you—gently but with all the enthusiasm of a kid in a candy store—to embrace this multilingual lifestyle with open arms. Don't view it as a checklist or a chore but as a vibrant, enriching part of your life that brings you closer to the vast, wonderful world.

Now for the action bit, the 'what comes next?' I want to light a fire under you to start or keep pushing forward on this incredible path. Grab the strategies we've explored, lace up those shoes tight, and confidently step out. Set your goals, keep that patience tank topped up, and remember: every challenge is just a stepping stone to your successive linguistic triumph.

Language learning, as we've discovered together, is an ever-evolving adventure. Stay curious, stay open, and let the winds of innovation fill your sails. As the world changes, so does how we can weave new languages into our lives. Be ready to adapt, explore, and grow.

I can't thank you enough for joining me on this ride. Your trust, time, and eagerness to dive into the pages of this book mean the world to me. I'm rooting for you, hoping the paths we've wandered together have equipped you with the tools and the fire to chase those multilingual dreams.

And hey, I'd love to hear how you're getting on! Your triumphs, your oops moments, the unexpected turns— sharing these stories can spark inspiration and courage in all of us walking this path. Let's keep the conversation going, supporting and cheering each other on as we unlock new languages and worlds.

Here's to you, the future polyglot. To the languages you'll conquer, the connections you'll make, and the incredible journey ahead. Let's make it legendary.

SHARING IS CARING!

If you love it, leave a review
and share with your friends!

Scan to leave your book
review

11

References

• *Consequences of multilingualism for neural architecture* https://behavioralandbrainfunctions.biomedcentral.co m/articles/10.1186/s12993-019-0157-z

• *Acriticalperiodforsecondlanguageacquisition* https://www .ncbi.nlm.nih.gov/pmc/articles/PMC6559801/

• *HowTheWorld'sTopPolyglotsLearnLanguages* https://stor ylearning.com/blog/methods-top-polyglots

•*MemoryTechniquesinLanguageLearning* https://ihworld.c om/ih-journal/issues/issue-38/memory-techniques-in-language-learning/

• *SMART Goal Setting For Language Learning – Linguasorb* https://www.linguasorb.com/blog/smart-language-goa ls

• *8BestLanguageLearningApps(2024)* https://www.wired.c om/gallery/best-language-learning-apps/

• *The benefit of immersive language-learning experiences ...* https://www.cambridgeenglish.org/blog/the-benefit-of-immersive-language-learning-experiences-and-how-t

o-create-them/
· *8 Time Management Tips for Students - Harvard Summer School* https://summer.harvard.edu/blog/8-time-manag ement-tips-for-students/
· *The Interleaving Effect: Mixing It Up Boosts Learning* https://www.scientificamerican.com/article/the-interl eaving-effect-mixing-it-up-boosts-learning/
· *The Complete Guide to SRS Language Learning - FluentU* https://www.fluentu.com/blog/srs-spaced-repetition-la nguage-learning/
·*The Crucial Role of Learning a Foreign Language in Context* https://www.languagesalive.com/the-crucial-role-of-le arning-a-foreign-language-in-context/#:~:text=Learn ing%20in%20context%20promotes%20long,skills%20i nto%20one's%20daily%20life.
·*ThePowerofMnemonicsinLanguageLearning*https://wor dtap.net/the-power-of-mnemonics-in-language-learni ng/
· *The benefit of immersive language-learning experiences ...* https://www.cambridgeenglish.org/blog/the-benefit-of- immersive-language-learning-experiences-and-how-t o-create-them/
· *The10BestLanguageExchangeSites*https://www.linguaso rb.com/blog/10-best-language-exchange-sites
· *8BestLanguageLearningApps(2024)*https://www.wired.c om/gallery/best-language-learning-apps/
· *The Benefits of Using Film in Language Learning with Memrise* https://www.memrise.com/blog/from- hollywood-to-fluency-the-benefits-of-using-film- in-language-learning-with-memrise
· *The IPA Alphabet: How and Why You Should Learn the*

International Phonetic Alphabet with Charts https://www.la
nguagematters.co.uk/the-ipa-alphabet-how-and-why-
you-should-learn-the-international-phonetic-alphabe
t-with-charts/
· *The Shadowing Technique: 7 Simple Steps for Successful ...*
https://www.fluentu.com/blog/language-shadowing/
· *Best6+AppsForPronunciation: YourPathToFluentSpeech*
https://ling-app.com/tips/apps-for-pronunciation/
· *Learning Language through Music: Science and Songs*
https://lingopie.com/blog/learning-language-through-
music/
· *The method of loci as a mnemonic device to facilitate learning*
... https://www.ncbi.nlm.nih.gov/pmc/articles/PMC40561
79/#:~:text=The%20method%20of%20loci%20(MOL,ar
range%20and%20recollect%20memorial%20content.
· *TheCompleteGuidetoSRSLanguageLearning*https://www
.fluentu.com/blog/srs-spaced-repetition-language-lear
ning/
· *These Memory Techniques Can Do Wonders for Your ...*
https://www.speaky.com/these-memory-techniques-
can-do-wonders-for-your-language-learning/
· *VisualsInTheLearningProcess-eLearningIndustry*https://e
learningindustry.com/unlocking-the-magic-the-transf
ormative-power-of-visuals-in-the-learning-process#:
~:text=Visuals%20enhance%20memory%20retention.,
V
isuals%20can%20even%20facilitate%20repetition.
· *How To Create A Language Learning Routine Without ...*
https://effortlessconversations.com/language-learning/
language-learning-routine/
· *The Benefits of Multilingualism to the Personal and ...*
https://www.ncbi.nlm.nih.gov/pmc/articles/PMC56621
236

26/
· *Are there Cognitive Benefits of Code-switching in Bilingual ...*
https://www.ncbi.nlm.nih.gov/pmc/articles/PMC74132
23/
· *23 Ways To Immerse Yourself In A Language Without ...*
https://www.babbel.com/en/magazine/ways-to-immers
e-yourself-in-a-language
· *Howartificialintelligenceisrevolutionizinglanguagelearning*
   https://www.berlitz.com/blog/artificial-intelligence-ai
   language-learning#:~:text=In%20recent%20years%2
   C%20technology%20has,dynamic%20and%20engaging
%20learning%20experiences.
· *Howartificialintelligenceisrevolutionizinglanguagelearning*
   https://www.berlitz.com/blog/artificial-intelligence-ai-
   language-learning#:~:text=AI%20enables%20personali
   zed%20learning%20paths,learner's%20proficiency%20
level%20and%20weaknesses.
· *Virtualreality-assistedlanguagelearning: Afollow-upreview ...*
      https://www.frontiersin.org/journals/psychology/artic
les/10.3389/fpsyg.2023.1153642/full
· *MultilingualismandGlobalCitizenship*https://www.un.org/
en/chronicle/article/multilingualism-and-global-citize
nship
· Tyabaev,A.E.,Sedelnikova,S.F.,&Voytovich,A.V.(2015).
Student-Centered Learning: The Experience of Teaching
International Students in Russian Universities. https://doi
.org/10.1016/J.sbspro.2015.11.578
· Global Assembly on the Climate and Ecological Crisis:
Evaluation Report. https://doi.org/10.57711/81rj-qb50
· PPT-CSD5400REHABILITATIONPROCEDURESFORTHE
HARD OF HEARING PowerPoint Presentation - ID:180602.

237

https://www.slideserve.com/Sophia/csd-5400-rehabilit
ation-procedures-for-the-hard-of-hearing
· A Luminary Adventure: Exploring LED Lighting in Quebec
| Grupoe Fex Brasil. https://grupoefexbrasil.com/a-lumi
nary-adventure-exploring-led-lighting-in-quebec/

www.ingramcontent.com/pod-product-compliance
Lightning Source LLC
Chambersburg PA
CBHW070920120626
46546CB00001B/343